PHIL MERRIC
LUCY WARD

FOOTBALL LEADERSHIP HANDBOOK

PHIL MERRICK
LUCY WARD

FOOTBALL LEADERSHIP HANDBOOK

How to get the best out of yourself and your team

DB PUBLISHING

This handbook covers all aspects of leadership and provides a model that everyone can use to ensure a consistent approach across your football club.

To be a great leader you need to know how to get the best out of yourself and the people you lead.

The best clubs have great leaders on and off the pitch.

We can all be leaders.

'This handbook provides an insightful and applied link between the effectiveness of leadership and group dynamics and its use goes way beyond the football environment.'

Ali Wareham – Head of A level PE
Peter Symonds College Winchester

For Oliver George

First published 2022 by DB Publishing, an imprint of JMD Media Ltd,

Nottingham, United Kingdom.

ISBN 9781780916361

Printed in the UK

ABOUT THE AUTHORS

Phil Merrick FInstLM

Phil is a Fellow of the Institute of Leadership & Management and a former senior executive with one of the biggest banks in Europe. He has managed complete businesses from sales through to back-office operations and his senior positions include head of group audit, head of business banking strategy, head of corporate programme management and head of asset finance operations. As well as spending most of his time in Chester, London and Edinburgh, he has been on assignments in Eire, France, Austria, Australia and New Zealand. Phil and his teams have reviewed the performance of numerous businesses and have led restructures, acquisitions, disposals, start-ups, closures and mergers.

On the sporting front, Phil was a successful semi-professional footballer on the North-Wales coast and managed teams including his local club Prestatyn Town where he was also chairman. Under his stewardship Prestatyn made Welsh football history by winning the Welsh Cup and reaching the Europa League second qualifying round in only his second season at the helm and their first-ever attempt in Europe. He has written books about the business of football and managed a golfer, who is now an Assistant PGA professional, and also a motor-racing driver, who became 2013 British Formula Ford Champion and 2015, 2016 and 2021 Porsche Carrera Cup Champion and raced in the BTCC. As a junior, Phil played basketball for Wales, football for North Wales and represented his county at cricket and athletics. Born in Leeds, he is a passionate Leeds United supporter, lives in North Wales with his wife Sian and has three daughters, Gemma, Hannah and Kate, and a grandson, Oliver George.

Lucy Ward

Lucy is a retired footballer who represented England U21 when she was just 16 years old. She joined Leeds United Ladies when it was a community team and stayed with the club as they rose to be one of the best teams in England, spending most of her career there, with one season at Doncaster Belles. Lucy played in the Women's FA Cup Final against Arsenal Ladies and scored at Elland Road in Lucas Radebe's testimonial, coming on as a substitute for Gary Speed, where she also set up a goal for Matthew Kilgallon.

Lucy was head of education and welfare at Leeds United's very successful boys' academy for 17 years, overseeing around 250 junior players and a number of young first-team players. She left the club against her will in 2015, winning a high-profile legal battle against Leeds owner Massimo Cellino over her unfair dismissal for sexual discrimination.

Lucy now works for the Premier League as an education support manager as well as a football commentator for broadcasters such as BT Sport, BBC, talkSPORT, Channel 4 and Sky. She has worked on World Cups, the Olympics and the Euros since 2007 and in addition covers Premier League games for Prime Video and BT Sport.

Lucy lives with her partner Neil Redfearn, two dogs and two ginger cats near Leeds.

FOREWORD

I've been involved in football at a senior level for a long time now, and I fully believe that it is the people and leadership that determine whether or not you are successful. And success of course means different things to different people. Winning the Champions League is a benchmark of success for the elite clubs, but so too is the level of support you might give to your community, your schools and your hospitals. I feel privileged to have been at the helm of an English Premier League Club, the best league in the world, and now looking forward to the challenge of getting there again, this time with Bolton Wanderers FC. Whatever league your club is in, the principles are exactly the same. It's about getting the right people doing the right things, with the key ingredient, *leadership*.

A football club of course is about results, and importantly the fans, and we owe it to them to do the job properly.

I first worked with Phil on the Burnley FC Leadership programme so have witnessed his philosophy on leadership first hand. He breaks it down into logical steps that anyone can follow, and that's the point, it is for everyone involved at a football club. Whether you are a coach out on the pitch or one of my fellow directors in the boardroom, we can all pick up something from this handbook.

Creating winning teams at your football club is not just down to the chairman, or chief executive, or manager, it is down to all of us – and it starts here, right now, with you.

Neil Hart – CEO Bolton Wanderers FC.

A PERSONAL NOTE FROM PHIL MERRICK, CREATOR OF THE •PEOPLEMAD MODEL:

Improving performance on and off the pitch.

Football is my sport. Having been a player, manager and chairman, I understand the business of football and how footballers think and behave. I also have a strong business background and have a track record of building high-performing teams, spending much of my career in trouble-shooting roles, helping businesses improve performance, particularly through the organisation and management of people.

This hands-on experience in business and sport, together with training from subject matter experts, not to mention hours and hours of study, has provided me with the knowledge and experience to write this handbook.

I am delighted that Lucy Ward has been able to help with the writing of this handbook, sharing her personal views and experiences. Lucy has fantastic knowledge of all aspects of the game both on and off the pitch and it is really interesting to see how she has used that expertise to develop a successful career in the media industry.

The **•peoplemad model** has been used to deliver leadership workshops to businesses, schools and English Premier League clubs.

It is important that everyone at the football club feels part of what is going on and that there is joined up thinking between what happens in the board room and what happens out on the pitch.

'The single most important thing for a manager is the relationship with the owner of the football club.'

Tony Pulis — football manager

'It all begins with a ball and a child. The ball is usually some kind of plastic/rubber compound (leather is for big kids) ...

'The child, of course, is flesh and blood, yet he or she is drawn to this artificial object, mesmerised by its shape and its unfamiliar smell. It looks solid and inert but as soon as it's nudged, a wonderful thing happens – it moves!'

Gianluca Vialli - from his book *The Italian Job*

'Your first club is always your best one, of course. It comes as a bit of a shock when they do not want you any more, and your second club suffers as a result. Finally I snapped out of it. The old cliché says that the club is bigger than the player, but suddenly it dawned on me that the game is bigger than the club as well. I was playing the game long before any club came for me, and my first loyalty was to football. I loved the game for itself. It did not matter what strip I was wearing, I went out to play football and to win. It was the only way I knew.'

Terry Venables – from his autobiography

ABOUT THIS HANDBOOK

Leadership should start at the very top of an organisation. These people should set the scene, the standards, the guiding principles, *this is the way we do things around here.* Everybody else then knows what's expected of them. This book covers all aspects of leadership at a personal level, team level and club level. It also covers the important area of career development which is a critical area for anyone involved in football. It's not just young enthusiastic academy players and seasoned professionals at the end of their playing days that need help. The turnover of management, coaching and operations staff is a frequent event at most football clubs.

The sections are in the logical order of the **•peoplemad model** and coded with an icon to help with navigation, as well as being an aid to remember the model and the leadership tips.

It is designed so that you can read it in page number order or simply dip into the relevant section for reference.

- Consistent approach to improving performance
- Important principles
- Simple techniques
- Easy to use and easy to remember

There are lots of leadership tips in this handbook, but as a minimum **remember these four and use them as basic rules for everything that you do.** They are explained in detail in the relevant sections.

1. Believe in yourself.
2. Work hard.
3. Surround yourself with the right people.
4. Keep things simple.

Hope you enjoy!

FOR ALL CLUBS EVERYWHERE ...

Whether your club is owned by a rich Arab Sheikh, a local businessman or a Community Trust run by the fans, the important ingredient that makes everything work is leadership. Having lots of money in theory gives you an advantage, but this is not enough without the ability to attract the best coaches and the best players. Importantly, the right people that suit your football club and your particular set of circumstances. Then you have to patiently build the team and create a winning environment.

The more leaders you have at your football club, the more successful your club will be. This is where you come in. Build your own leadership skills while helping other people to do the same.

Do it for yourself.
Do it for your colleagues.
Do it for your football club.

This handbook is written for everyone at a football club, from grassroots upwards. Naturally, depending on your role and the status of your club, some of the points may be familiar, but the important point is that all sections are complimentary and work best when used as a model.

'The quality which sets apart the very best from the rest is leadership.'

Howard Wilkinson - football manager and Chairman of the LMA

OXFORD ENGLISH DICTIONARY DEFINITIONS

Coach

- Train or teach as a coach.

Manage

- Be in charge of.
- Run.
- Supervise (staff).
- Be the manager of (a sports team or performer).
- Administer and regulate (resources under one's control).
- Maintain control or influence over.
- Succeed in surviving or attaining one's aims.
- Cope.

Lead

- Be in charge or command of.
- Show someone the way to a destination by going in front or beside them.

Teamwork

- **To come together to achieve a common goal.**

Get everyone passionate about the goal!

'Football is easy. Life is complicated.'

Pelé

CONTENTS

Lucy Ward's notebook can be found throughout the hand book giving her views based on personal experiences on and off the pitch.

Note: all sections can be applied to everyone at a football club unless specifically notated:

Board room / Operations

Boot room

AT THE END OF EACH SECTION THERE IS A BRIEF SUMMARY OF THE KEY THINGS TO GET RIGHT.

1. THE •PEOPLEMAD MODEL

Get the right mindset.

Develop your strategy.

Surround yourself with the right people.

Get the right people doing the right things.

Create an environment that breeds success.

Build capability for you and your team.

Get everyone behaving as leaders.

IT STARTS WITH YOU TAKING CONTROL

It's about you.

You are at the heart of the model – you control everything. Think of yourself as the conductor or the ring master. In charge and in control.

The model has been designed in this format so that it's easy to understand, easy to remember and importantly easy to implement. We think in pictures and a model gives structure and order on which to build future knowledge.

Albert Einstein said that doing the same thing over and over again and expecting different results is a sign of madness. It follows then that to improve performance (moving from where you are today to where you want to be tomorrow) you need to do something differently. This particularly applies to the way you think – improving performance and being successful is directly linked to the application of thought. How you think is critical in helping you achieve your goals. In **•peoplemad** everything revolves around you. This is your model and it starts with getting the right mind-set.

The methodology in very simple terms:

- Believe in yourself. Know what you're aiming to achieve and get the right people on board.
- Get them doing the right things in an environment that will allow them to flourish and perform at their very best.
- Build your own and your team's capability and get everyone behaving as leaders.

2. MINDSET

Get the right mindset.

Having the right mindset is critical for improving performance.

Thinking is a skill. Be great at it.

MINDSET: THE THEORY

- You are the centre of your own universe.
- You control your own thoughts and your own actions.
- You have your own beliefs, objectives and ways of doing things.
- There are over **7 billion** other people doing exactly the same.
- There will be **10 billion** long before the end of this century.
- Lives are bound to clash.
- There will be conflict.
- There will be accidents.
- There will be competition for what you are trying to do.
- Accept this is how it works, that's life. Your success will come from how you deal with it.
- Learn to understand:
  - how other people think
  - how other people behave
  - the impact you have on other people.
- *It makes sense to be really good at dealing with people.*

That's why the model is called **●peoplemad**.

'The man with the best mind wins.'

Gary Player - champion golfer

Lucy's notebook:

Within my career, I was around at the time when women's football was moving from amateur/enjoyment to professional. There was a lot of resistance to this change from volunteers within the game who didn't want it taken from their grasp. This was one of the big reasons why it took a lot of years to become fully professional. Change of mindset was key to this transition and the elite players at the time drove this change through their attitude towards being the best regardless of not having the resources to be fully professional. Along with the FA and their great work led by Hope Powell, this then impacted and influenced the next generation.

'A great football team is the right balance and the right mixture of players. Good leaders, good communicators and good technicians. You need people that are strategically astute. People need passion, desire and most importantly, a willingness to keep learning.'

Hope Powell CBE – international football manager

BELIEVE IN YOURSELF

- I'm a big believer in having a positive attitude. Not to the detriment of reality - I don't believe for a second that we live in a perfect world and everything is pink and rosy.
- I'm positive because I believe you can make things happen.
- A lot of what happens in life is of your own making.
- Don't complain, don't make excuses, don't blame your circumstances and certainly don't blame other people.
- How can you expect other people to believe in you if you don't believe in yourself?
- Attitude is everything.
- You can achieve what you believe.
- **Especially if you want it badly enough.**

- What would you do if you knew you couldn't fail?
- What would you do if you didn't care what people think? Would you do things differently? What's stopping you?

> ***Self-belief is the key to driving performance and getting results. It is easy to believe in yourself when results are good. When things aren't going so well it is the Self-belief that will help get things back on track. Keep the belief.***

'I have seen so many top players with potential come through and not quite make it because their mentality wasn't right. I've seen others get through because they had the mentality even if they didn't have the ability.'

James Milner – football player

Lucy's notebook:

I worked closely with James Milner at Leeds United, and along with Lewis Cook he had the best mindset of all players I have worked with. His attitude to everything he approached was the same whether it was football or education. James was well aware that it would become increasingly difficult to switch mentality off the pitch to on the pitch. This is one of my key messages over the years to young players in my care.

How you are in a classroom in terms of your personality characteristics is how you are on the pitch.

I could predict what sort of players the lads were from teaching them without seeing them play. It is virtually impossible to be lazy about education and then be fully 'on it' when it comes to training and playing football. This doesn't mean that you have to be an academic high-flyer, but you need to give the best and have that work ethic to everything you approach.

KEEP THINGS SIMPLE

- Things that are overcomplicated can be difficult to understand and even more difficult to explain to someone else.
- The more complex something is, the more chance there is of it going wrong and the more difficult and costly it will be to put right.
- Things do not have to be complicated to be effective – very often it's the opposite.
- Experts in process design understand that almost all quality improvement comes from simplification of design, layout, processes and procedures.
- Keeping things simple especially needs to be applied to communication, which needs clarity and understanding for it to be effective.
- De-clutter: your life, your way of working, your coaching methods, in fact get rid of anything that can get in the way and slow you down. Get rid of things that are not important. Both physically *and mentally.*

You need to be continually aware of your team's ability to listen, understand and carry out instructions. Everyone is different. For example, players with too much to think about will not perform at their best. Over complicating tactics can work against you.

'It was easy to play for Liverpool because their philosophy was that football is simple.'

Kenny Dalglish – football player and manager

TAKE CONTROL OF YOUR THOUGHTS AND ACTIONS

You control how you think.

Everything is in your head. Everything. Your ideas, your emotions, your beliefs, your worries, your memories. Your whole life is played out inside your head and you have the power to determine how you live it. You decide who you listen to, what you read and what you believe. You have complete freedom over what you think.

You decide
- **How you think**
- **How you behave**

You already control the two things you need to be successful.

You control how you behave.

You control your behaviour. No one else. The actions that you take and the things that you say are entirely within your control. How you react to different situations and how you treat other people is entirely down to you. *Life is about making choices, success is about making the right choices.* **You decide whether you get up in the morning and take on the world or stay in bed. It's your life, it's your choice.**

Don't let other people control your thoughts

- Be careful who you listen to.
- *Be careful what you believe.*

LOSE THE WORD 'FAILURE'

- Don't talk about failure.
- Don't even think about it.
- The word does not have a place in the **•peoplemad** vocabulary.
- We don't fail, we try different things.
- If something doesn't work out we learn from it and do it differently next time.
- Stretching yourself and pushing the boundaries inevitably means that everything you try will not work out.
- That's how you discover things. That's how you learn.
- How do you know how good you could be if you don't reach the point where you don't succeed?
- If you believe you will achieve your goals at some point in the future and accept that you will have setbacks along the way, then each set back is one step closer to achieving those goals.
- Don't be afraid of making mistakes.
- Push, try, learn, push, try, learn ...

'A key factor to performing well in sport (and life) is your ability to control the quality and quantity of your internal dialogue.

You need to stop yourself from stopping yourself.'

Garret Kramer - sports psychologist

HOW HIGH CAN YOU GO?

A good analogy is the pole vault where they raise the bar to a new height every time you clear it. If you keep raising the bar at some point you will knock it off.

This is not failure.

This is seeing how high you can go.

- Push the boundaries.
- Stretch yourself.
- Try new things.
- Meet new people.
- Discover yourself.

Remember this when giving feedback to your team.
Effort and trying your hardest is to be commended at all times irrespective of whether or not objectives are achieved.

'If at first you don't succeed, try, try again. If at first you do succeed, try something harder.'

PM

Lucy's notebook:

Losing the word 'failure'

I think it is a real game changer when you get to the point in your life where you realise that failure doesn't exist, it is just life experience. It doesn't kill you; it just allows you to learn. It is so important that people learn this as early in life as possible to allow maximum development in their chosen field.

How high can you go?

In terms of pushing boundaries and comfort zones, it is something that I have challenged myself to do, particularly in later life (I wish I had the confidence to do it earlier in my career!). This has all been around my broadcasting journey and the large leaps outside my comfort zone when I have debuted on Olympics/World Cups/Euros over the years to an audience of four million plus in some cases. The buzz you feel from pushing your boundaries is incredible and even though you're not always perfect it is better than staying comfortable in my opinion.

THINK *OUTCOME*

- **You**
- **Event**
- **Outcome**

Y+E=O

In it's simplest form, life is about you, your relationships with other people and the various outcomes that happen as a result. That's all there is.

•peoplemad is about you taking control and improving those outcomes.
Decide the outcome you want.
Improve your capability and learn how to work with and get the best out of other people in order to achieve it.

This stamp is used throughout the handbook as a reminder – make sure your actions deliver the right outcomes.

Get into the habit of thinking 'What OUTCOME do I want?' You can then work backwards to see how you are going to achieve it. This way of thinking is very powerful, you can apply it to anything.

It is particularly helpful when dealing with conflict and learning to control emotions (Emotional Intelligence).

Event – pause – think what outcome do I want? – act.

GET THE RIGHT ATTITUDE

Attitude is infectious, is yours worth catching?

Attitude comes from beliefs. Beliefs stir feelings and emotions, and when you feel strongly about something you will behave in a way that reflects those feelings. Religion ... feeling wronged ... a cause you feel strongly about ... your football team.

So, if you want to change someone's attitude towards something then the only sure way of doing it is to try and change their beliefs – which is actually very difficult.

If you can get everyone on your side believing in what you're doing then you've cracked it ... and it's a great feeling when there's a common goal and every one is excited and enthused by it. Some people will go to extraordinary lengths to support something they believe in.

Always look for the right attitude first and foremost when you're recruiting people because you can generally teach people how to do the job (given the right skills etc) ... it's very difficult trying to change someone's attitude.

A word of caution: make sure you can spot the difference between confidence and arrogance. **Confidence is good, arrogance is dangerous.** To improve performance you have to continually look at what you're doing and see if you can do it better. Arrogant people think they know everything already and are not interested in what other people have to say.

They only look in the mirror to admire themselves, not to question themselves.

'On some occasions the will to win is more important than the skill to win.'

Gerard Houllier - football manager

Lucy's notebook:

I looked after Kalvin Phillips throughout my time at Leeds United. He entered the Academy system relatively late at 14 when most of his peers had been at the club since seven or eight. For the many cons of getting into a pro club late there are a lot of pros. The main one being that you don't feel the pressure that is built up for years inside a young player that he must get to be a scholar at 16 and if he doesn't it is a 'failure'.

Kalvin held none of that baggage, he just loved every minute of being at his home-town club and the chance that he had to train and play there for however long that would be, he didn't care! He was so laid back which actually allowed him to cope with the pressure. Don't get me wrong, he had lots of ups and downs after he was given his debut by Neil Redfearn in 2015 as the club was pretty unstable at the time, yet he kept going and working hard, taking the luck and opportunity given to him further down the line by Marcello Bielsa.

'An absolute honour and dream come true to be able to represent England at a major tournament like this. I'll give my all to make this country proud.'

Kalvin Phillips - football player

WINNING MENTALITY

The Oxford English Dictionary definition is:

- Winner: a person or thing that wins.
- Mentality: characteristic way of thinking.

- Winning people have winning ways – they know what's needed to be a winner.
- Winners inspire other people to be winners.
- Winners are positive people – they don't think about failure.
- Winners usually have high energy levels and a desire to get things done.
- Winners who have tasted success want more of it.
- Winners hate losing - 'show me a good loser and I'll show you a loser'.

'When I don't win I cannot be happy and I cannot change that in my DNA, and I hope I can influence the players to not be happy without winning football matches.

If you are happy by losing football matches it is difficult to be a winner. In any moment of your career that's the basic principle.'

José Mourinho - football manager

'Make the best of every situation.'

PM

MAKE THE RIGHT CHOICES

- Life is about choices.
- Success is about making the right choices.
- Remember - your beliefs determine your attitude.
- Your attitude drives your behaviour.
- So, believe in what you're doing and you'll do the right things.

Attitude plays an important part in building personal capability in Section 7.
This is the differentiator between success and failure.

'I asked myself – do I aspire to be good or do I want to be the best?'

Alessandro Del Piero - international footballer

'I know there's a lot of things that have been said about me, but I have to stay humble, I have to keep learning, I have to keep my feet on the ground.'

Buyako Saka - football player

SOME THINKING TIPS

Declutter

- Get rid of the things that get in the way of your plans and slow you down.
- Both physically AND mentally.
- Keep things simple.

Don't worry about the wrong things

- Don't worry about things you can do nothing about.
- It adds no value whatsoever.

Don't fret

- If you don't like something, change it.
- If you can't change it.
- Change the way you think about it.

Don't dwell on the past

- Life is like a book. You'll never move on to the next chapter if you're still re-reading the last one.

'I decided I can't pay a person to rewind time, so I may as well get over it.'

Serena Williams - grand slam tennis player

'I've always been fascinated by intelligence and how our brains work, and how they can be improved.'

Clare Balding - presenter

Lucy's notebook:

Don't worry about the wrong things

Not worrying about things that aren't in your control is difficult. I look at people's opinions of me when I am commentating (for example). What others think about you is none of your business ... so hard to adopt but actually is the truth. When people comment directly to me on social media it is hard not to get upset when it is nasty and conversely you shouldn't get carried away when there are good comments.

If you stay somewhere in the middle you will cope with any eventuality in your career.

'If I walked on water, my accusers would say it is because I can't swim.'

Berti Vogts - German football player and ex-Scotland manager

Always be positive

- The body does what it's told by the brain.

Whether you think you can
Whether you think you can't
You're right.

Always be self aware

- Think about what you do.
- Assess how well you do it.
- *Ask yourself if you can do things better.*

Be true to your values

- Do the right thing.
- Always.
- Even when no one is watching.
- Because it's the right thing to do.

Make things happen!

I am, I can, I will.

'Pride, passion, work ethic, belief, respect, honesty – they can hold a group together. As a minimum this is what we stand for.'

Sean Dyche - football manager

Lucy's notebook:

Doing the right thing – even when no one is watching

I read a book by Anson Dorrance about his work with the NC Tar Heels back in the day when they were the top basketball team in the USA. He talked about champions working hard when no one is watching. That resonated with me, I have met so many people who talked a good game about how they trained or how much revision they had done for an exam. I used to be in awe as a youngster but the older I got and the more I trained but didn't tell the world about it I realised it was about doing not talking about doing.

Interestingly, Anson Dorrance found that he had to work at bringing competitiveness into training as due to the interaction in women it is not something that comes naturally. He would set up competitions and duels between players at every stage of training so they could never shy away from that aspect and it became second nature. And guess what? As soon as it became second nature they became the best.

'What you do when no one else is looking will determine how good you'll be.'

Anson Dorrance - American soccer coach

MINDSET IN SUMMARY

KEY THINGS TO GET RIGHT

- Believe in yourself.
- Keep things simple.
- Take control of your thoughts and actions.
- Lose the word 'failure'.
- Think 'outcome'.
- Get the right attitude.
- Make the right choices.
- Declutter – physically and mentally.
- Don't worry about the wrong things.
- Don't fret.
- Don't dwell on the past.
- Always be positive.
- Always be self aware.
- Be true to your values.

3. STRATEGY

Develop your strategy.

Neil Warnock's advice to a new manager:

'Make sure you get a good Chairman or owner.'

STRATEGY: THE THEORY

You don't jump on a bus without knowing where you're going and what time you're likely to arrive, so that should be the same with your team.

Do you have a vision? Are you excited by it? Are you passionate about it? Importantly, are your team excited by It? If they are and they believe in what you're doing then you're a long way towards having a happy, motivated team. People perform better when they feel good about themselves and feeling part of what is going on and contributing is very motivational.

Of course you need a plan.

A vision without a plan is nothing but a dream.

You will be able to get your plan from a gap analysis between the picture you draw about today (known as current state in project land) and the one you draw about tomorrow – your vision. List the things you need to change, put them in some sort of order and this will be your plan of action.

Importantly, be honest with yourself about what life looks like today. If you pretend things are better or worse than they really are then you will not come up with the right list of things that need attention or be able to accurately prioritise the things to tackle first.

It is the same for personal development. You won't be able to plan where you want to be in a few years time if you don't have a vision of where that place is and what it looks like (this is covered in more detail under Capability).

OVERARCHING STRATEGY

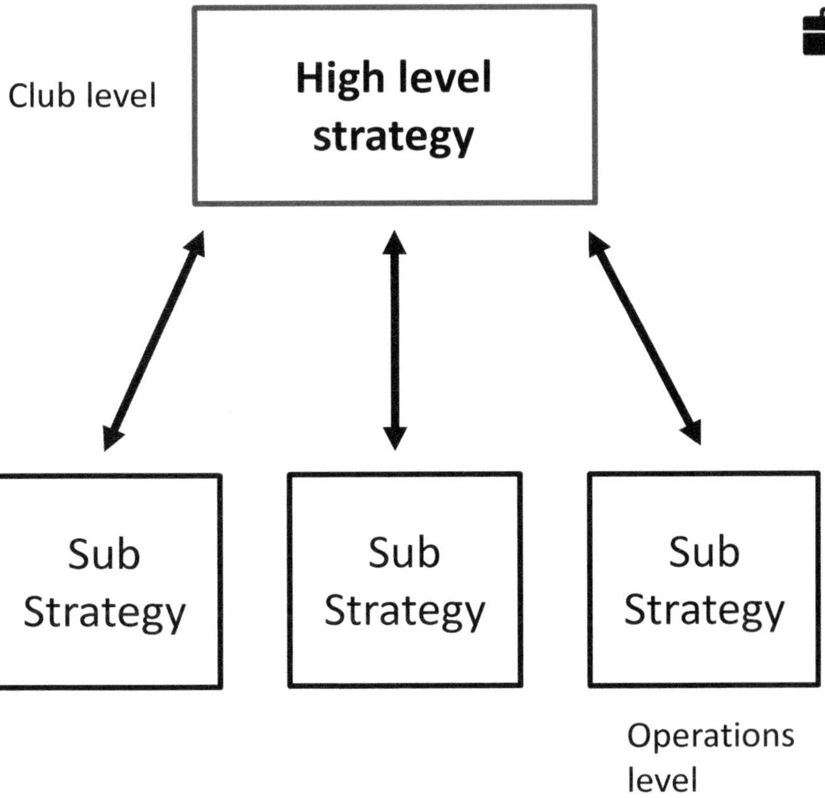

The ideal situation is that there is one overarching strategy at club level and the different playing and non-playing teams have their own strategies that support it.

The important point is that ALL sections of the football club are heading in the same direction, guided by a single strategy.

STRATEGY IN SIMPLE STEPS ...

Knowing where you are today, knowing where you want to be tomorrow and having a plan to get there.

- Picture the future – your vision.
- What will success look like? Define what the future will look like in words, figures and pictures. Show what you will achieve with your strategy.
- Check today's position – your current state assessment.
- Devise how you can move from today's position to achieve your future vision – your strategy.
- Set yourself some targets and objectives.
- Work out what you are going to do and when – your plan.
- Put your plan into action – the execution.

Note: Execution. You can have the best strategy in the world but it is a complete waste of time if it's not carried out properly. Make sure you get the right people, doing the right things, in the right environment; which of course are key elements of the ●**peoplemad** *model.*

'Unfortunately it became clear that those at the top of the club did not share the same vision.'

Rafael Benitez - football manager, on leaving Newcastle United

CREATE YOUR VISION

- Aspire, desire, dream.
- Open your mind.
- Don't put restrictions on your thoughts.
- Believe you can do anything that's physically possible.
- Research it.
- Draw it.
- Write it down.
- Give it as much detail as possible.
- Sleep on it.
- Close your eyes and paint it in your mind.

Check and rationalise

- Are you passionate about it?
- Can you get excited by it?
- Why are you doing it?
- **Is it within reach? It doesn't have to be easy but it needs to feel achievable to keep you motivated.**

Have a shared vision with everyone in your team.

Believe in it.

Be passionate about it.

Get everyone bought into it.

'We have the power to change lives with our drive, ambition and relentless positive attitude.'

Neil Hart – when CEO at Burnley FC

Vision

Think it.

See it.

Draw it.

Write it down.

Want it.

Believe in it.

Don't lose sight of it.

Be clear what you want and how you're going to get it.

The clearer the detail the easier it will be to achieve.

Otherwise you risk doing the wrong things.

GET BUY-IN FROM YOUR TEAM

When you are developing your strategy, there can be huge benefits to involving people who can help you achieve it. Apart from contributing to the discussions, your team will feel involved and it gives a sense of ownership when you're putting your plans into action.

- Teamwork is about being involved and, importantly, feeling involved.
- Think of the people who will help you realise your vision.
- Do you need to involve people who will be impacted by your strategy? (Possibly different people to those who will help you achieve it.) Whether you include them or not will depend on how they are impacted.
- Start with your vision.
- Brainstorm ideas.
- Take your thoughts and drawings and turn them into detailed descriptions of what the future looks like.
- Plot how to move from today's position to the vision.
- Get commitment and support as early as possible.
- Assess the risks and put mitigation plans in place.

'Rome wasn't built in a day, but then again I wasn't on that job.'

Brian Clough - football manager

ASSESS WHERE YOU ARE TODAY – IN DETAIL

Knowing where you are today:

- See Section 7 for ideas on personal strategy.
- Carry out a review – a *current state assessment.*
- Understand today's position in as much detail as possible. This will vary according to your responsibilities but as a minimum should include strengths and weaknesses of yourself, your staff and your players. Think of all the factors that ultimately affect your success directly and indirectly.
- Assess everything including people's feelings and, importantly, behaviour.
- Get accurate facts and figures.
- Be truthful as to the realistic position.
- The more accurate and detailed the information, the easier it will be to make decisions on what needs to change.
- This is about today – forget any current plans to change things, don't cloud the issue with what might happen in the next few days, weeks or months.
- Think of it as a snapshot in time.

The things to consider in this exercise will obviously vary across the different areas of the football club.

Critical in all areas, however – your people.

Lucy's notebook:

These days players who are signed on Scholarship agreements complete a Sporting Excellence Professional apprenticeship (SEP) which is externally assessed through an end-point assessment. The thread that runs through the SEP is the players assessing their start point looking at their progression and seeing where they end up in that two-year period. And this is on all aspects of their role as a footballer. Technical/tactical/physical/psychological/communication/ career development to name a few. There's a reason for this: it allows a starting point and then an opportunity to create a plan to get where they want to go. I think that it allows players to learn to look inwardly and critique their level and recognise their targets.

For a 16 to 18-year-old player these are excellent skills to learn and develop.

CREATE YOUR PLAN

- Take the vision and compare with the current state to see which areas need to change.
- Make a simple plan – a list of what you are going to do and when.
- If you need the help of other people then also decide who is going to do what.
- The more people involved and the more complicated the change being undertaken then the more detailed the plan will need to be.
- Some activity will depend on other things that need to be done first – in project management these are called dependencies.
- Think of the risks involved – they will need to be managed and they take time.
- Think of the people involved – they will need to be managed and they take time ☺.
- All plans have financial implications – think costs and budgets and align financial plans to operational plans based on activity and timelines.
- Make sure you consult whoever is responsible for your club's finances – **before** taking any action.
- Plans need to be kept up to date and communicated.

Always remember the three key variables when planning:
time, quality, cost.
If you change one of these it is likely to impact one or both of the others. E.g. if you want to do things quicker then it could cost you more or you may have to compromise on quality.

NOTE: PLANNING CAN BE EASY

- Make a list of all the things that need to be done.
- Put them in some sort of order, remembering that some things might be dependent on others (e.g. if you are building a house the walls can't be built until the foundations are in).
- Draw a timeline and put the actions that need to be taken under the appropriate dates.
- Allocate jobs to people.
- A trick is to start with the end date and work backwards. It's like planning a journey. What time do I want to get there? How long will it take? So what time do I need to leave?
- Put in some milestones – where you want to be by a certain point in time. This will help target progress and give a sense of continual achievement.
- Sit back and assess whether your plan is realistic and achievable under your timescales.
- Have I missed anything?
- What would happen if?
- Plan, plan and plan again until you are happy.
- Planning is a skill, be good at it.

Think OUTCOME

The simple trick of starting with the end date and working backwards might seem obvious but you would be surprised how many people don't do it.

Note: strategies and tactics need to be continually reviewed in line with changing circumstances.

PAUSE AND REFLECT

- Build some breathing space into your plans, a couple of days every month or so. It is a good discipline to sit back and check that everything is on track – there is nothing wrong with building in pauses.
- It also helps with contingency – just in case your plan needs a bit more time in certain areas.
- No matter how well you plan there will be things that come out of the woodwork and affect your timelines.
- Rushing to squeeze things in might seem okay in terms of meeting your plan, but it is high risk and could affect the quality of your work.
- Think about consolidation – depending on what it is you are doing there may be an occasion where you want to pause to let things settle down. Get people acclimatised, let your plans bed in a little before moving on to the next stage.
- In very big projects involving large-scale change, chunk up the work, deliver, pause, embed, check it works, move on to the next bit.

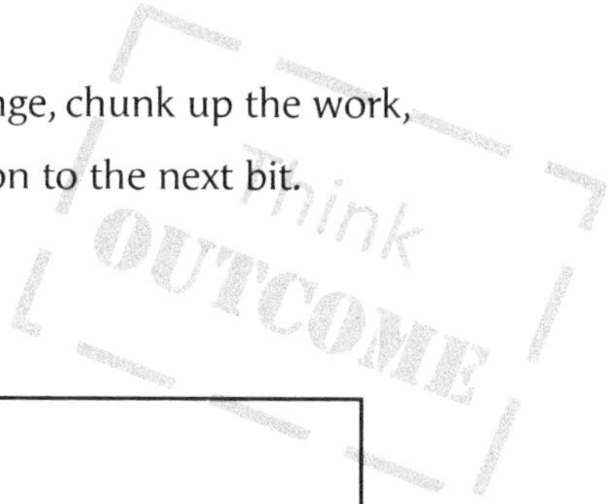

Think if ... then, if ... then

- *Take a step back and review your plan.*
- *Every action has an outcome.*
- *Check your plan to make sure all the actions deliver the changes that you want to happen.*
- ***If we do this then this will happen.***

PRIORITISING TASKS

- Make sure that you get the right balance between time spent planning and the time spent doing things.
- Don't rush into things – you will make mistakes and waste a lot of time undoing or correcting things.
- Efficiency is about doing things in the right order at the right time for the right length of time, and this needs planning.
- The flip side of this is that you don't want to spend too much time deliberating where to start. Every second you spend planning is not being spent on taking action.
- In a competitive situation you could be leaving a window of opportunity open for someone to 'get in there first'.
- A quick way to prioritise tasks is to tackle the important ones first and the ones that are the easiest to carry out – see diagram.

> *If things are desperate and urgent action needs to be taken then think how do I plug the holes in a sinking ship? This will quickly identify what needs doing first, then when you've stopped the leaks you can move on to all the other things that need doing.*

It is interesting to note that some clubs have appointed strategy executives e.g. Everton and Manchester United. The roles vary in content and look at different aspects of the football club, including the effectiveness of the academy and the quality of management information.

PRIORITISE YOUR TASKS

Create an action plan starting with what's important and relatively easy to implement.

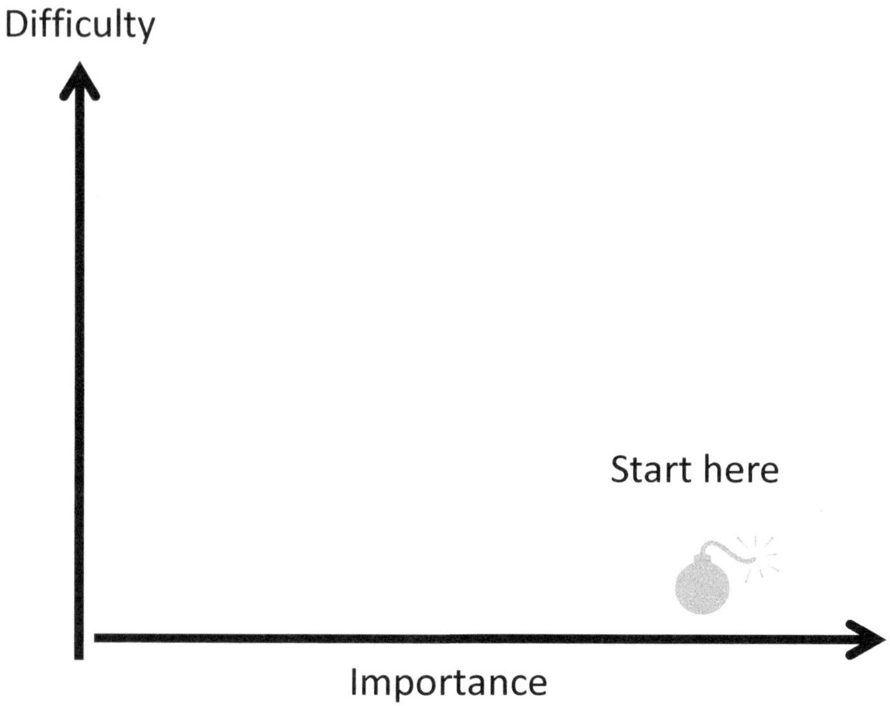

What's important?

What's easy to action?

Start with what's important and easy to action.

Get the quick wins.

SET YOUR GOALS

The Oxford English Dictionary definition is: *an aim or a desired result.*

- You now have a vision and a strategy – setting goals will give focus to make it happen.
- In many businesses the terms goals, objectives and targets are often used interchangeably. For simplicity, in this handbook the term 'goals' is used to describe the desired outcome and is considered to be a combination of targets and objectives.
- **Targets are what you are aiming for, objectives are the things you achieve along the way to help you get there.**
- Keep objectives simple and attainable.
- Make sure they are the right ones and lead you down the right path.
- Describe them in such a way that there is no doubt when they are achieved.
- **Set some short-term objectives – they will act as stepping stones and give a sense of achievement along the way.**
- Get commitment and support – think about everyone impacted by your actions.
- Communicate progress.
- **Celebrate success as each objective is achieved.**

Make your objectives SMART:

- *Specific*
- *Measurable*
- *Achievable*
- *Realistic*
- *Timely*

Think OUTCOME

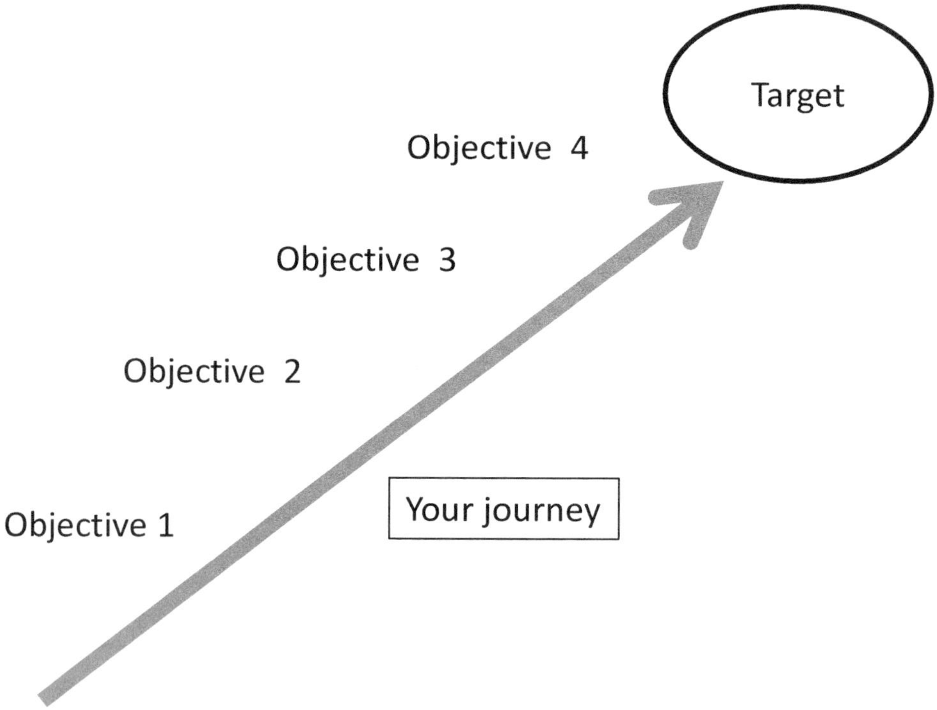

Focus on the future.

It's no use worrying about the past. You can't change it so just learn from it.

You can change the future so that's what you should focus on.

YOUR JOURNEY – HIGH-LEVEL STRATEGY

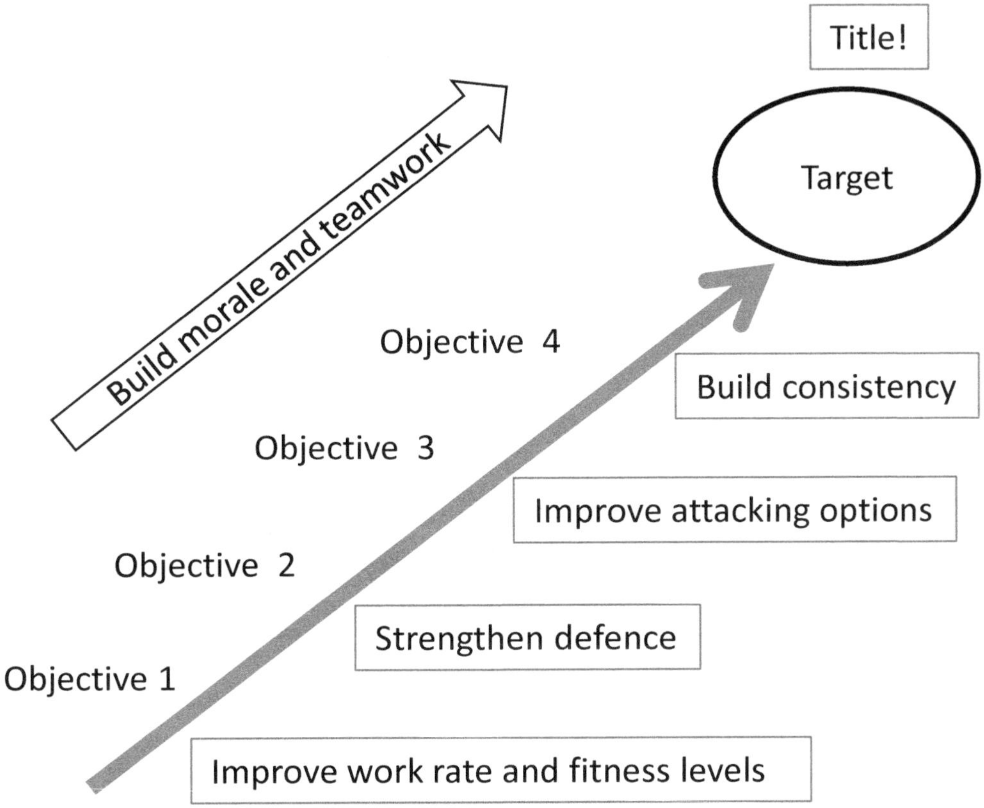

A very simple example of a high-level strategy that could be adopted when taking over a new side. Behind each one of these objectives is the need to continually review personnel and make sure you have the right people with the right skills, experience and, importantly, ATTITUDE.

How *you achieve these objectives, of course, will need a great deal of thought, rigorous planning and* ***effective leadership skills****.*

SOME STRATEGY TIPS

Understand the difference between tactics and strategy

- Tactics – short term.
- Strategy – long term.

Think:

- *Tactics to win the battle.*
- *Strategy to win the war.*

Think:

- *Tactics to win the match.*
- *Strategy to win the league.*

Note: games are never won on the tactics board. The best tactics in the world are useless if they are not executed properly. You need the right people doing the right things in the right environment. With the right leadership.

Be clear about your aims

- Be absolutely clear what you are doing and why you are doing it.
- Think of the risks.
- Think of the people.
- Think of the impact.
- *Think about the benefits.*

'People don't succeed because they're lucky. They succeed because they set goals and work toward those goals. They plan for success.'

Unknown

EXECUTE EFFECTIVELY

- Execution is about implementing your vision and strategy, putting your plans in place and making things happen.
- This is the essence of the •**peoplemad model**:
  - Surround yourself with the right people.
  - Get the right people doing the right things.
  - Create the right environment.
- Execution will be a combination of carrying out your normal day to day business activity and a series of projects designed to deliver your strategy.
- In simple terms, projects differ from *business as usual* in that they have a start and end date and a specific set of deliverables that need to be completed within those dates.
- Projects impacting the business will need time to bed in – the integration of projects into business activity needs careful thought and planning, especially the impact on people.
- You want the best people all focused on delivering the strategy, working hard in an environment that allows them to flourish.
- Don't underestimate how hard it is to get this right. Strategy is nothing without effective execution.

Remember the principles of basic planning:

- *Decide the actions to take you from where you are today to where you want to be tomorrow.*
- *Plan what you need to do and when.*
- *Work backwards fitting everything in.*
- *If it doesn't fit, change the amount of work to be done or the end date.*

Lucy's notebook:

Clarity of message is supremely important in my line of work, both through football and broadcasting. Using live TV as an example, as a producer or director you need to get your message across quickly and concisely and it has to land in the way that you intend. There are no second chances.

I could talk for ages about the unbelievable high skill level needed to be a top-level director/producer and presenter of live football on TV. I have worked with some of the best and its not until you do it or observe it that you realise how hard it is. Imagine someone talking in your ear whilst you are presenting to camera, thinking of what to say and what you can ask your guests. There will also be a countdown going constantly in your ear where someone is telling you how long you have left to the next VT or the commercial break.

Gabby Logan, Jake Humphrey, Clare Balding, Gary Lineker, Nat Quirk, Helen Skelton have all shown me the high level they work at with all that going on in their ear. So spare a thought for that next time you notice a small mistake or how masterful and relaxed they seem.

MEASURE PROGRESS

- This is covered in more detail in section 5. It is important that you keep on top of your plans.
- Stay ahead of the game.
- Always measure progress towards achieving your targets and objectives.
- Checking progress should be a routine. Put it in the plan.
- Remember to use milestones to check that you are up to where you need to be – as per your plan.
- Continually re-assess whether your plan is realistic and achievable under your timescales.
- Once your plan is underway, keep abreast of new data, events, issues etc that affect what you are doing.
- Flex your strategy and plans in line with changing circumstances.
- It is okay to re-plan.
- Plan, plan and plan again until you are happy.
- Will we deliver everything?
- Will we meet our timescales?
- Communicate progress. Communicate, communicate and communicate again until you are absolutely sure everyone has got it!

Celebrate success

- *Feel good about achieving your goals.*
- *Enjoy the moment.*
- ***It keeps you wanting more.***

IMPACT ON OTHER PEOPLE

- Whenever you are making decisions and taking action, it will invariably affect other people.
- Think about the impact you are having on other people's lives and emotions.
- Remember that you need other people to make things work.
- Think about what you say and how you say it.
- **Be honest.**
- If you are uncomfortable delivering difficult messages then seek advice, and get training.
- Giving good messages needs as much preparation and attention as giving difficult messages.
- Always think 'how will this make people feel?'
- When you communicate with someone, always consider 'how do I want them to feel? What do I want them to do about it? It helps you choose the right words.
- Remember people perform better when they feel good about themselves.
- **These points hold true for everyday life situations but are magnified in times of change.**

See Risk Management in section 6.

Remember: continually flex strategy and tactics in line with changing circumstances. Be ahead of the game, on and off the pitch. Know what's going on at every level of the football world, the league, other clubs, your club, your staff, your players and especially your fans.

Lucy's notebook:

One thing that I've mentioned in this handbook is how your actions are perceived by others. Try to get in their head and see how they feel, given their experiences, about how you are behaving and the decisions you are making. I try to be like that in every day life. I think that empathy is underrated and for some reason in the modern world is seen as a weakness. I disagree entirely with that. Whether you are trying to make people work hard for you as the leader of their team or whether you are just trying to understand a person's behaviour, empathy is one of the biggest strengths you can have. People will always remember how you made them feel emotionally and it is a powerful thing to be able to affect others in a positive way. Happy people make better players in an academy system. Dealing with issues and teaching kids to know how to recognise and deal with issues is imperative. My role at Leeds was 'everything but the football' but without 'everything but the football' the players would not have got through. A training ground develops a player whether that is the laundry worker who listens to a lad who talks through his problems with his new girlfriend, to the physio who might recognise signs that not all is well at home. All these people play a part in an academy that produces good people as well as good players. Every cog is important and my welfare role was to pull all this together.

OVERALL OBJECTIVE

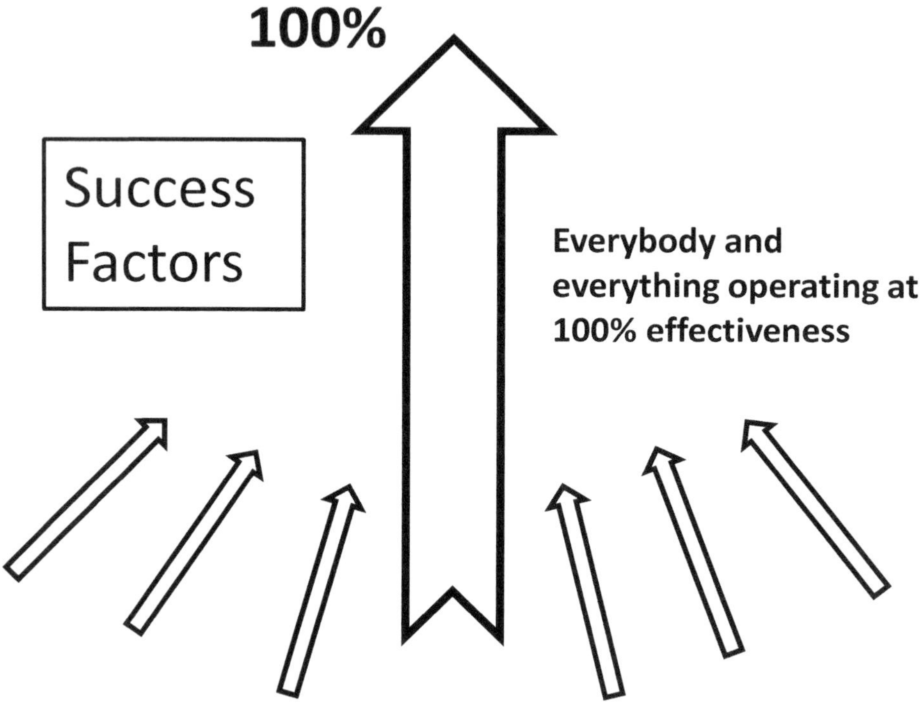

100% BELIEF › ATTITUDE › ACTION

Find your success factors

Really think about the key things that will make you successful.

What are they?

Where are they?

Who are they?

Get them all working at 100 per cent.

STRATEGY IN SUMMARY

KEY THINGS TO GET RIGHT

- Create your vision – be clear what you want.
- Get buy in from your team.
- Assess where you are today – in detail.
- Create your plan – a gap analysis of today vs tomorrow.
- Prioritise your tasks – start with important and easy.
- Set some objectives and use as stepping stones towards your vision.
- Celebrate success as each one is achieved.
- Understand the difference between tactics vs strategy.
- Continually flex strategy and tactics as things change.
- Measure progress.
- Execute effectively – right people, jobs, environment.
- Think about your impact on other people.
- Get your all your success factors working at 100 per cent.

4. PEOPLE

Surround yourself with the right people.

Other people affect your happiness and success.

Choose them wisely.

PEOPLE: THE THEORY

- No matter how self-motivated or independent you are, you need other people.
- You rely on other people every day of your life. Thousands of actions taken by friends, relatives, customers, politicians, employers, colleagues, suppliers, coaches, teachers, mentors etc impact your life and how you feel.
- How many bad days have you had because the train was late, a delivery didn't arrive, your phone signal was down or you were late because of those infernal road works?
- The better other people are at doing their jobs the better your life will be.
- This is particularly evident in a team situation where you are dependant on your colleagues.
- If you are in a management position your performance will be determined by how well other people do their jobs.
- People are powerful creatures – we communicate, create things, have ideas, make decisions, *we make things happen.* We influence other people.
- Other people have attributes that you don't have – why not use their skills to complement yours?
- **The power of many is a lot more than the power of one.**

> *People are the most important asset in any football club and more important than computer systems, stands, pitches, training facilities etc because these things don't build or look after themselves. In life we are influenced and impacted by the people with whom we choose to spend our time.* ***Choose them wisely.***

GET YOUR RECRUITMENT RIGHT FIRST TIME

The model is called **●peoplemad** for a reason. You are who you mix with.

Life, business and football is about building relationships and dealing with other people. That's all there is. Just reflect for a second – most of our lives are spent speaking to, listening to, playing with or watching other people.

You don't do business with companies – you do business with the people who work in those companies. The outcome will be determined by your relationship with those people.

Make sure you are good at relationships because people deal with people they like dealing with.

How much time do you spend on people matters?

How much time do you waste on people matters?

There is a huge difference.

How many people do you recruit, train, coach, mentor, appraise, discipline and then eventually have to let go? Lost man hours, wasted effort, huge costs. 'Get it right first time' needs to be applied to recruitment.

To get it right first time choose people with the right:

- Attitude (critical)
- Personality (they need to interact with other people)
- Capability (skills, experience and knowledge)
- Potential (you will need to invest in development and be prepared to wait for performance to improve over time).

'You're only as good as your players.'

Neil Lennon - manager of Celtic FC on being named Scottish Premier League Manager of the Year, May 2012

Lucy's notebook:

The best managers/leaders I have worked with use the best parts of their teams' skills. In essence they use the tools they have so they succeed and the team succeeds. There is no shame in admitting something isn't your strong point – you cannot be good at everything. We got it right at Leeds because we had a strong female influence in the academy when other clubs didn't and I think it made our kids better humans and in turn better players. Stacey Emmonds (strength & conditioning) Faith Atack (physio) Mary Lally (academy secretary) and myself allowed us to challenge any behaviours that weren't appropriate in a softer way.

Young male players usually only have two types of women they know of: family matriarchs and girls that they meet online or out socialising. I found they didn't have that 'professional' woman role model. We offered that and the lads didn't know any different to how they had been brought up. That was until we would go to other clubs to play U18s games and myself, Stace and Faith would be part of the match-day staff. We would get comments from the opposition coaches 'would like to work at your club with those three blondes…' and our lads would literally turn round and look confused with the penny finally dropping that they were talking about their S and C coach, their physio and the person who looked after them. Now that, in my eyes, was progress. We were producing young men who recognised females in management positions that weren't a surprise or a token gesture. They didn't know any different, how powerful that was.

RECRUITMENT TIPS

- Entice the best people to apply and pick from a big pool.
- Only recruit the right person to the role.
- Don't 'make do' because there is no one else. The best of a bad bunch is still bad.
- Remember people have potential and will develop with the right encouragement and development.
- You are responsible for the welfare of the people you recruit – help them, make sure they are happy in their work, give them the tools to succeed.
- **Take ownership – you are responsible for the performance of the people you employ. If it doesn't work out you are still responsible.**
- Beware of arrogant people because by their very nature they don't look at themselves to see if they can improve.
- Don't confuse arrogance with confidence, which is an attribute.
- **Spotting the right people is a skill – be good at it.**

> ***'What's been key in every deal we have done is knowing what players will bring to the club from a mentality point of view as well as a technical and tactical point of view. Strong characters, strong personalities, good people. We are in a situation now where all of those boxes have been ticked, but it started down in League One.'***
>
> **Chris Wilder - manager, Sheffield United**

- You need people who will help you achieve your objectives and help you live your life as you want it to be.
- It is important that people should complement each other – they don't have to be like each other.
- Ability is important – having the right skills, knowledge and experience.
- Having the **right attitude** is critical.
- Don't surround yourself with clones of yourself or people who are afraid to challenge what you do and say.
- **Always pick the best person for the job, irrespective of creed, gender or race.**
- See people as a force.
- It is impossible to be an expert on everything – focus on what you do best and get the help of the experts for everything else.
- Be careful not to prejudge based on first impressions – it's amazing what you can discover and learn from people from all walks of life.
- **The quicker you get the best people on your side the quicker you'll get there.**

Surround yourself with the right people.
Make it a rule and stick to it.

'If you want to be a great manager, get great players.'

Steve McLaren - football manager

Lucy's notebook:

Recruitment is key. It can be the difference between success and failure. Good managers benefit from good players. Diversity of thinking is one of the main factors I look at in decision making. Have you got people on your team who think differently to you? That has to be a yes otherwise you end up doing what you have always done. For us at Leeds it was the female voice and brain which gently questioned any dinosaur thinking. It got the men thinking about how they were as colleagues and leaders of these young men. I questioned staff all the time. Why are you doing this/ that? Gave them info about the players they were looking after so they knew why behaviour might not always be good. I had one young player who just couldn't or wouldn't behave in school. Discipline seemed the only answer and that wasn't working. The area that he came from and then some info I learned about his childhood experiences were not conducive to a good start in life. You have to get on the lads' level, you have to find an 'in'. Luckily over the years I have developed good skills to enable me to do this. Respect has to come from the adult first and it is amazing where that gets you with this type of kid. When they see that you will run through brick walls with them they will eventually lead the way. What I never tolerated was dishonesty and lads taking the mickey out of me and advantage of my actions. They were told this at the start and I never needed to shout, the lads ended up not wanting to disappoint my faith in them. It's a long road but it is so fulfilling.

CHANGING PERSONNEL

- Change happens. Sometimes it is forced upon us through sickness and injury, people leaving etc, and sometimes it is planned such as termination of contracts.
- **Change is always disruptive** and needs managing. It not only impacts the way you run things it can also impact the rest of your team in terms of feelings and behaviour.
- Making a small change is easier to manage. If it was planned in order to improve things then it should be relatively easy to check whether or not it produced the desired result. If you make lots of changes then it becomes much more difficult to see what worked and what didn't.

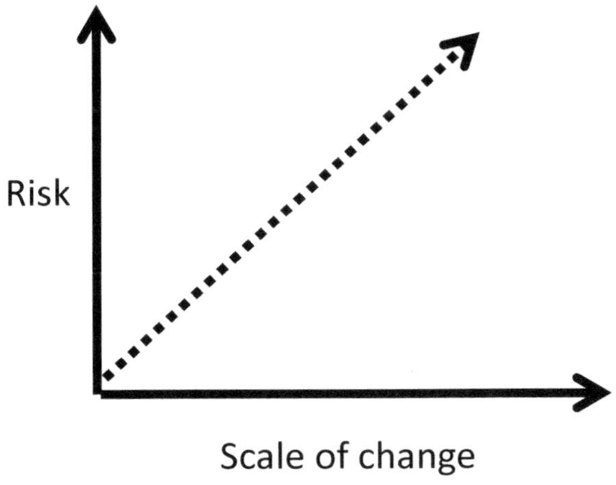

The bigger the change, the greater the risk.

Lucy's notebook:

During our time in the LUFC academy, Neil, myself and the staff always built teams that would benefit individuals. We found that rather than concentrating on certain players that we thought would 'make it', Neil built a team at U18 and U23 level that would bring the best players to the fore but also maximise the potential of the players that would be released.

Importantly, this meant that all players benefitted from their time in the academy.

Far too many academies just rely on working on the cherry-picked ones and hoping that they progress, narrowing the opportunities for more to excel. One player may surprise you through this method and psychologically it allows all players to genuinely think that they have a chance to progress. Lots of success with players through this method: Charlie Taylor, Sam Byram, Lewis Cook, Lewie Coyle, Kalvin Phillips, Alex Mowatt, Bailey Peacock Farrell, Alex Cairns to name just a few.

CHANGING PERSONNEL - TEAM MANAGEMENT

- Team management is knowing how to get the best out of everyone and by playing them in the positions that work best for the team. Right people, right jobs.
- Using the risk model on the previous page, it follows that making too many changes to your team increases the risk of not performing as well as expected.
- Having a settled team allows players to get used to playing with each other and understand each others' strengths and weaknesses.
- Obviously there will be reasons to bring in new players and rotate the squad – lots of games in a short space of time, giving squad players playing time, bringing through youngsters from the academy, tactics on the day etc., but changing the team too much will usually have negative results.
- If you look at successful teams of the past you can usually name the starting eleven and the key members of the squad.

It helps if you can recruit players who are versatile and can play in more than one position. If there are injuries or suspensions then they can slot in without disrupting the overall structure of the team. James Milner for Liverpool in recent times and Paul Madeley for Leeds United in the 70s are great examples of players who were prepared to play in any position for the benefit of their team.

Change takes time and the amount of time needed will depend on the scale of change. Unfortunately, in a results-based business a lot of chairmen are not prepared to give coaches the time they require to properly build their own teams, in their own style with the type of players they need to suit their own particular brand of tactics.

Frequently changing managers with different views on how the game should be played means that you never get to a place of having a settled team with a common sense of direction.

The practice of frequently sacking managers can also have a serious negative effect on someone's mental health. Apart from continually worrying about pleasing people and making sure results go the right way, there is the huge stress that comes when the sacking actually happens.

What will people think?
Will I be able to feed my family?
Will I get another job?

'The telephone call confirmed everything. All the feelings and instincts developed over twenty-five years in the game told me this was my moment of truth. It was a call from Ken Friar, Arsenal's Managing Director, to discuss the day's business after I had finished training. Halfway through our conversation, Ken suddenly said: "Oh by the way, the Chairman would like to see you at 9 am tomorrow".'

Terry Neil - on being sacked by Arsenal in 1983

A call that every manager dreads. To this day the situation has not improved; in fact, it has probably got worse.

If you recruit someone and have to fire them then you need to have a long hard look at your recruitment process.

And it should hurt! After all, you decided they were right for the job in the first place.

A lot of football chairmen just don't get this. It happens all the time in the football world; here are just a few examples:

- By the summer of 2014 new Leeds owner Massimo Cellini had sacked his 36th manager in 22 years at his Italian club Cagliari.
- Chelsea had nine managers in six years before reverting back to Jose Mourinho, who they'd previously sacked.
- Spurs manager Tim Sherwood was given an 18 month contract, did a good job and was sacked after five months.
- Valencia CF. had six coaches and six sporting directors in six years!

Apart from being disruptive and all the other negative elements related to this sort of practice, there's also the huge financial cost of terminating contracts. David Moyes, sacked by Manchester United after just ten months, is reported to have been paid millions in compensation, as was José Mourinho just a few years later.

The circumstances are different for each club of course, but it's usually because the chairman/owner is desperate to improve results and bows to pressure from the media and importantly the fans.

This emphasises the point that people can be very powerful, especially as a group with passion, strong beliefs and a common cause, like their football team.

EXAMPLES OF SHORT MANAGERIAL REIGNS

Bob Bradley	Swansea	84 days	11 games
Frank De Boer	Crystal Palace	77 days	5 games
Rene Meulensteen	Fulham	75 days	17 games
Tony Pulis	Sheffield W.	45 days	10 games
Brian Clough	Leeds	44 days	8 games
Les Reed	Charlton	41 days	8 games
Alex McLeish	Notts Forest	40 days	7 games
Paul Scholes	Oldham Athletic	31 days	7 games
Paul Hart	QPR	28 days	5 games
Micky Adams	Swansea	13 days	3 games

It's accepted of course that each club has it's own unique set of circumstances and the reasons for the swift departures may well differ from club to club. The point is that changes like this can be far reaching for everyone involved, with serious repercussions operationally and financially.

Sometimes you can get the new manager 'bounce' effect which acts as a temporary lift but generally speaking any major change requires a step backwards before moving forwards because of the disruption and change in working practices.

Good people are hard to find. Look after them.

THE CONUNDRUM OF COACH OR MANAGER?

The creation of the director of football role (sometimes called sporting director) first rose to prominence in European football. Whilst the role varies from club to club, usually the main part of the job is to oversee player recruitment.

The question then is how much influence does the manager have any more over which players are bought and sold?

If the answer is none, then he is essentially a coach who is given the resources he has to work with. The coach does the best he can with what he's been given.

Personally, I couldn't work like that. I'd have to have a say about who was in my squad. I'd need to assess attitude and whether I could work with them. To be fair most clubs these days have a strong working relationship between their director of football and head coach.

The director of football role makes sense in that they can oversee the development of young players in the academy, run the scouting network, keep tabs on football agents, wheel and deal in the transfer market, as well as trying to keep abreast of the spiralling value of players and the corresponding costs of contract negotiations. This allows the head coach to do what he does best – work with the players.

This is a big change from the traditional football manager who got involved in everything football related. Sir Alex Ferguson is a great example of this when he was manager at Manchester United.

The best teams have the best players. If you are accountable for results then you need to have a say in who is in your team.

SURROUND YOURSELF WITH WINNERS

When we talk about surrounding yourself with the right people, then surround yourself with winners.

'I want to go unbeaten this season and win the league but if you lads are not going to do it for me then I'll go out and get someone who will.'

Don Revie - manager Leeds United FC

- *Winning people have winning ways.*
- *Winners inspire other people.*
- *Winners are positive people.*
- *Winners have energy and desire.*
- *Winners hate losing.*

'The most important thing is the end result and that's winning.'

Mick McCarthy
- international football player and manager

Lucy's notebook:

Through my experience with women's football, the USA national team is the ultimate example of a winning mentality.

Technically the players may not be the best ones, physically they are collectively the best (this has set them apart over the last 30 years, although other countries are now catching them up) but their seemingly inbuilt will to win takes them that final important step.

This goes back to Title IX in the 70s which gave equal opportunities in sports to all children, female and male alike, so much so that 'soccer' is not laden with the 'male sport' tag in the states like it has been historically in the UK. (The FA banning womens' football for 50 years in the 20s didn't exactly help of course.)*

The team are competitive and driven and this as a collective overrides everything and drives them to success. They are infectious with each other.

Title IX of the Education Amendments Act 1972 is a Federal law that states: no person in the United States shall, on the basis of sex, be excluded from participation in, be denied the benefits of, or be subjected to discrimination under any education program or activity receiving Federal financial assistance.

DON'T STIFLE INITIATIVE

The Oxford English Dictionary definition is: *The ability to initiate or begin something;* On one's own initiative: *without being prompted by others.*

- People with initiative:
  - Have 'get up and go'
  - Think for themselves
  - Don't wait to be told what to do
- Initiative stems from inherent enthusiasm.
- People with initiative don't need pushing – they need guiding and controlling.
- Initiative comes from a desire to take action.
- Initiative is a great quality in someone – don't stifle it with too many procedures and rules.
- Encourage, praise, and monitor.*
- **Caution*** – there is a risk that people with initiative do the wrong things if they don't wait to be told what to do.

There are three types of people:

- *Those who make things happen*
- *Those who watch things happen*
- *Those who ask 'what happened?'*

Recruit people with the right attitude.

Don't compromise or it will cost you dearly.

BELIEFS

The Oxford English Dictionary definition is: A *firmly held opinion or conviction.*

- If you feel strongly about something you will behave in a way that reflects those feelings (religion, a cause, feeling wronged).
- This is because your beliefs determine your attitude towards something which then drives your behaviour (see section 2 Mindset).
- A simple example of how it might work for a football fan:
  - Belief: the manager of your football team is not good enough
  - Attitude: you have lost all faith and want him out
  - Behaviour: you join in protest marches and chant anti-manager songs during the match.
- It follows that in order to change someone's behaviour the best way to do it would be to change their beliefs.
- This is a powerful subject and plays a big part in improving personal performance – believe in what you're trying to achieve (See section 7).

'It's important for everyone to follow their passion, be driven by ambition and what you want to become in life.'

Andrea Radrizzani – chairman Leeds United FC

Lucy's notebook:

Players attitudes have a massive effect on the success of the team. It is precarious managing a football team as you have to manage people who are playing and those who aren't playing.

I have seen a large number of first-team players over the years at Leeds United whose attitude has affected the performance and attitude of the team even when they weren't playing. It is that important.

As a manager you have to do all you can to remove these energy sappers from the environment you are trying to create. At Leeds, for a period of time players like this were allowed to affect the environment at the club – it has a devastating effect and is difficult for the rest of the staff and players to function properly.

Neil Redfearn always used to say you are only as good as your senior players.

BELIEFS: VALUES AND MORALS

The Oxford English Dictionary definition:

- Values: *principles or standards of behaviour.*

The Oxford English Dictionary definition:

- Morals: *principles of right or wrong.*

- Values and morals are beliefs about behaviour and what you perceive to be the difference between right and wrong. They are put together here because they both determine attitude.
- Attitude drives behaviour – people feel strongly about their values and morals and are rarely prepared to change – which means the same behaviours will continue.
- If your team has shared values and an agreed code of behaviour, they are more likely to gel and get on with each other.
- Trust comes from an understanding of each other's values.
- Don't try to inflict your beliefs on other people – they have as much right to their beliefs as you have to yours.

'Killed and betrayed by the people I appointed. I am a man of principles.'

Sepp Blatter - former president of FIFA

TALENT, SKILL, KNOWLEDGE, EXPERIENCE

The next few pages are things to consider when recruiting people but also apply to your own development. It goes without saying that successful people need ability and having the right talent, skills, knowledge and experience to do the job is an absolute must.

The better other people are at doing their jobs the better your life will be – especially in a team situation.

If you are the manager you'll be judged on how well your team performs.

Make sure you use people to their full potential. If you don't get the best out of someone and don't use all their skills to best effect then you're losing out. **Twice**. *You're not getting full benefit from that person because you're not fully utilising what's at your disposal and your costs are higher than they need to be. It's a waste of valuable resource. Also it's not fair on the person; high achievers want to be stretched and challenged.*

'I know my players better than anybody and I am the biggest supporter and fan of all these players.
These are the ones that I've signed, these are the ones that I've worked with day in, day out. They don't always get it right but I know the strengths and weaknesses in their personalities as well, and what works for one might not work for the other.'

Chris Wilder - manager Sheffield United

TALENT

The Oxford English Dictionary definition is: *Natural aptitude or skill.*

- Some people are naturally gifted at doing certain things.
- It is no coincidence that talented children often have talented parents, but it is not necessarily about their DNA.
- Starting at an early age, having purpose, hours of practice, the best tutorship and a belief in your own ability all foster this 'natural' aptitude.
- Whether talent is a gift or something that is learned, it still needs to be nurtured and developed.
- You will have talents that other people don't have – use them to your advantage.
- Other people have talents that you don't have – use them to your advantage.
- Talent is wasted if it is not married with the right attitude and application.

'I like beautiful football better than pragmatic football, and if you can play well you have more chance of winning things.'

Marcelo Bielsa - head coach, Leeds United FC

SKILL

The Oxford English Dictionary definition is: *The ability to do something well.*

- You will be good at something if you:
  - Have the best coach/teacher
  - Learn the right technique
  - Work hard
  - Believe in yourself
  - Yearn to be the best you can
  - Practice, practice, practice
  - Don't give up.
- Watch other people who already have that skill.
- Dealing effectively with other people is a skill. Make this skill important to you.
- Give yourself the advantage – **be able to do something better than everybody else.**
- Work at it, practice, practice, practice.

'He taught us how to trap a ball coming at us with our chests, or our shoulders, or our thighs, or even our feet. He impressed on us one thing that even today few coaches take the trouble to teach, and that is what to do before the ball comes to you...... Valdemar taught us to stand sideways to the ball until the last minute.'

Pelé - talking about Valdemar de Brito

KNOWLEDGE

The Oxford English Dictionary definition is: *Information and skills acquired through experience and education.*

- Make sure you have the right knowledge aligned to achieving your objectives.
- Do things.
- Read things.
- Learn things.
- Write things down.
- Get interested in different things.
- Ask questions.
- Be more interested in other people than you are in yourself.
- The more knowledge you have the more you will be able to apply common sense to decision making. This saves time and is key to improving performance.

People make things happen.

Imagine great people all working at 100 per cent.

With 100 per cent quality.

For 100 per cent of the time.

With the right skills, knowledge, experience and ATTITUDE.

'If you're the smartest person in the room, then you're in the wrong room.'

Confucius

EXPERIENCE

The Oxford English Dictionary definition is: *Practical contact with and observation of facts or events.*

- This should be broader than just having experience in the job in hand.
- The more you do, the better informed you will be.
- The better informed you are then the easier it will be to make the right decisions.
- Experience in subjects unrelated to your objectives is still an important experience.
- Experience doesn't come from age, **it comes from doing things**.
- Get out there and do things – including travel (not just abroad) to see different people and cultures.
- Get as much experience of dealing with people as you can possibly get.
- Read more, ask more questions.
- Get interested in other people.

'When I was at Liverpool it was always about the players. If you've got a good fill of senior pros then you've got half a chance.'

Graeme Souness - footballer, manager and TV pundit

COMMON SENSE

The Oxford English Dictionary definition is: *Good sense and sound judgement in practical matters.*

- Common sense can be considered an essential skill and will be continually improved through knowledge and experience.
- Success is about making the right decisions more often than you make the wrong ones – this requires sound judgement.
- A practical approach helps to 'keep things simple' – a requirement of **peoplemad**.
- Common sense is the ability to think rationally which helps in pressure situations and when decisions are needed to be made quickly.
- Taking a 'common sense' approach to most things can save time and energy – eliminating the need for in-depth research and analysis.
- **Your gut feel is usually right – check it out, test it, learn to use it.**
- Practice, practice, practice.

> ***'At the start of a new season there are three simple objectives I love to achieve as quickly as possible. I look for the first goal, the first point and the first victory. Clinch the hat-trick in your first game and you're flying.'***

Howard Wilkinson - football manager, chairman of the LMA

WORK ETHIC

The Oxford English Dictionary definition is:

- *Work: activity involving mental or physical effort done in order to achieve a result*
- *Ethic: set of moral principles.*

- People with a strong work ethic believe that working hard is the right thing to do – it is one of their values.
- Talent alone is not enough – success needs hard work.
- Skills have to be learnt – they only improve with practice, practice and more practice.
- Successful people are not afraid of hard work.
- The 'work smarter not harder' saying should be 'work smarter and harder'.
- Make hard work a value for you and your team.
- Find a job you enjoy doing and it won't seem like hard work.
- **Caution** – 'All work no play' is dangerous. It is important for people to find the right 'work/life balance' that works for their own personal circumstances (see section 7 *Work hard, play hard*).

'The easiest thing to work on is your work rate.'

Ole Gunnar Solskjaer
- manager Manchester United

Lucy's notebook:

I have loads of examples of excellent players who didn't work hard enough and didn't make a career out of football and players who were nowhere near as talented but had that real work ethic so excelled their counterparts. And then utopia where a player was supremely talented and worked just as hard. Lewis Cook was in that last category – exceptional player, person and work ethic.

Kalvin Phillips joined the academy late (U15) so was never saddled with the pressure that is built up over the years from U9 onwards where kids (and mainly parents) were desperate to gain a scholarship at the club. Sometimes the players had fallen out of love with football but felt they had to keep going as their parents had given time and money over the years to reach the player's end goal. Kal just enjoyed every single minute at his home-town club and that laid back attitude helped his progression. Don't get me wrong he was driven and desperate to be a footballer but it wasn't the end of the world if he didn't. This has been a huge advantage for him.

Working hard in training and games costs nothing and is all about mindset.

POTENTIAL

The Oxford English Dictionary definition is: *Having the capacity to develop into something in the future.*

- Developing potential is rewarding and helps to improve team performance as people continually improve their own individual performances. It helps with camaraderie and team bonding. The alternative is to replace them with somebody better, which could be beneficial but can also be disruptive and costly.
- Everyone has potential, not everyone has drive
  - Can they improve?
  - Do they want to improve?
  - Are they prepared to work at it?
  - How good can they get?
  - Can you afford to wait?
- Get good at spotting the people with potential.
- Get good at spotting the people with potential **and the right attitude**.

> *Remember, attitude is everything.*

'Seven of those Barcelona players tonight came through the ranks of their club and that helps to make them an unstoppable force.'

Gary Neville
– football player, manager and TV pundit

PERSONALITY AND CHARACTER

Different people obviously have different personalities. Whilst the relevance of this point will depend on a person's role within the club, there is no doubt that a person's personality is key to building an effective team.

> The Oxford English Dictionary definition is: *The combination of characteristics or qualities that form an individual's distinctive character – lively, engaging qualities.*

- People deal with people – you want your people to be able to engage confidently with other people.
- Can they make eye contact?
- Are they comfortable making conversation?
- Are they interested in other people?
- Do they smile?
- You can often read a person by their eyes.
- **Do you like the person? If you don't there is a good chance other people won't either.**
- Learn to read body language.
- Get good at reading people.
- Listen to what they mean not necessarily to what they say.

'If you ask any youth coach in the world which were the ones that came through, it was always the ones with the best character.'

Tom Vernon
- founder of the right to dream football academy

Lucy's notebook:

I've had loads of different types of characters progress from the academy into the first team and they all shared a steely nature where they reacted really well to setbacks however big or small.

That was innate but also learned through a good environment of staff and older players.

'I can't keep up this hard image. I must be the nicest person I know.'

Vinnie Jones

– football player and Hollywood film star

SENSE OF HUMOUR

The Oxford English Dictionary definition is: *The ability to appreciate or express humour.*

- Laughter is an enjoyable experience – it raises spirits and makes people feel good about themselves.
- Being able to laugh at things releases tension.
- Humour is a big part of team camaraderie.

- CAUTION:
  - Team camaraderie often involves 'mickey taking' – there is a limit to what is acceptable and must not be cruel and divisive
  - Work must be taken seriously and humour must not detract from the job at hand.
  - Always respect your colleagues, their workloads and their personal circumstances.

- You need to be able to laugh at yourself – it helps with team spirit.
- Work hard, play hard, have fun.

'Judging by the shape of his face, he must have headed a lot of goals.'

Harry Redknapp - on Iain Dowie

Lucy's notebook:

Working in a professional football club training ground is an enjoyable experience every single day. Even when things are the worst they can be at a club, there is always laughter at the training ground as that is the energy that gets players and staff through their day. You have to be quick witted and thick skinned with the banter but you will always laugh.

At Leeds there were some awful moments (-15 points at the start of League One with Dennis Wise as manager, the club under the ownership of Cellino) but every day you would laugh and smile and that is what keeps the club going.

'He looks as if he should be surfing in California, and if there's one thing that annoys me about him, it's the tan. We haven't been to Barbados lately, so he must have been on the sun bed. As we approach February I like players to have that drained, pale look that I've always had at that stage of the season.'

Martin O'Neil - Leicester City manager talking about Robbie Savage

CHOOSING YOUR LEADERS

- Choosing the right manager/captain/supervisor is a critical part of helping a team deliver the right results.
- They must have the right attitude and ability.
- They must display leadership skills.
- They must be good with people.
- They represent you.
- You need someone you can trust.
- This is a form of delegation:
  - Be clear about your expectations
  - Discuss your strategy, plans and tactics
- You can delegate responsibility for managing/captaining/supervising the team but you must remain accountable.
- Stay interested, monitor progress.
- Continually give feedback on how well it is being done.
- Being in charge of other people can be an effective part of someone's development programme.
- Offer help and advice where needed but allow people the chance to show what they can do for themselves.
- Don't stifle them, support them with an open hand.

'Gift plus work plus talent plus the attitude, that's the cocktail for success.'

Gerard Houllier - talking about Steven Gerrard

A WORD OF WARNING

Off the pitch:

- Make sure they are available when you need them.
  - Try to match the working hours of your manager to those of the team.
  - Managing people is time consuming. They must be able to do their own job effectively and find the time to manage their team.
- Choose someone who is physically located in the right area.
  - Managing a team remotely from a different geographical location is not as effective as it would be if you were working alongside your team.
- Don't reward good performances by making people managers/ supervisors.
  - Your leaders should be chosen because they are capable of being good leaders.

On the pitch:

- Don't assume a good player will make a good manager. Managing requires a completely different set of skills.
- Your captain needs to play in a position where he/she can influence results.
- Make sure giving the captaincy to someone doesn't become a burden and spoil their own performance.

The captain represents the manager and is key to motivating and giving instructions to the rest of the team. I'm always wary of goalkeepers being captains because they're often too far away from the action. I'm fine with having 'keepers as club captains of course.

Lucy's notebook:

Players do not always make good managers but having experience as a player when it gets to the nitty gritty of a losing dressing room at half time when good decisions need to be made is vital to making those decisions.

Build your people skills and combine it with your playing experience and you're on the way to being a good coach/ manager.

'Some parts of the job I did very well, but not the key part of getting players to win football matches.'

Kevin Keegan – footballer player and manager talking about his failure at being the England manager

BRIEF NOTES ON ASSESSING PERFORMANCE

- Start an assessment with an open mind – clear your head of any pre-conceived ideas.
- Whilst your gut feeling is usually right, be careful not to let it influence your approach to the assessment. There is the risk that subconsciously you will try to prove your gut feeling right.
- Do your assessment and assess it fairly and rationally – then check to see if your gut feeling was near the mark.
- Use a rating system that suits you – the traffic light system in section 5 is quick and can be as accurate as you want it to be. Importantly, it's simple to use and prioritises what you need to focus on, which is the whole point of the exercise.
- Record brief notes as to why you've given the scores.
- Keep it simple.
- Continually monitor the success of your rating system and adjust it accordingly.
- Assessment is made easier if you have something to assess against – e.g. previous expectations, targets, objectives.
- Refresh your expectations after each assessment.
- Spend your time wisely: **performance is improved with action not analysis, which is just a means to an end.**

'It turns out that the two most powerful words in the English language are "Well done".'

Sir Alex Ferguson - football manager

SOME ASSESSMENT TIPS

- Give support to those who might be experiencing difficulty. Encourage. Have patience.
- Be careful about being dismissive of people who can't improve any further – they are actually performing at their peak and may still be invaluable to your team.
- Be careful not to promote for the wrong reasons – **Remember good footballers don't always make good managers – the roles have an entirely different set of skills.**
- Be careful if appointing a player-manager. Can they really concentrate on playing and managing at the same time? If so, make sure you appoint a really good assistant to give the right level of support.
- Try and get the right blend of youth, experience and talent across the team. Develop from within and if necessary supplement with experience brought in from outside.
- See section 5 for notes on how to manage performance.

Make assessment part of your regular routine

- Perform, measure results, give feedback, *improve* ...
- Perform, measure results, give feedback, *improve* ...

Make feedback instant

If you're doing the wrong things today then you don't want to be doing the same things tomorrow.

KEY LEADERSHIP TIPS

- Treat everyone the same: **with empathy, respect, dignity.**
- Good people are hard to find – look after them.
- Continually improve the quality of your people:
  - Planned growth through learning and development.
  - The introduction of new people who can meet the required standard or have the potential to do so.
- Succession planning is critical, **on and off the pitch.** When people leave it is disruptive. When somebody good leaves there is a risk that performance will be adversely affected, even if it's only temporary.
- Listen closely to what people talk about and how it's said – it's a clue to their personality
  - Do they talk about themselves or other people?
  - Do they dwell on issues or are they generally upbeat?
  - Are they talking at you or are they engaging you?
  - Do they have a purpose to the conversation or are they rambling?
- Watch out for big egos – there's no place for them.
- **Take action immediately if you have the wrong people.**

Deal quickly with bad behaviour

Deal with behavioural issues immediately they arise.

Don't ignore them and hope they'll go away.

Bad behaviour can become the norm and spread to others if it's not dealt with effectively and quickly.

It also shows it won't be tolerated.

Be true to your standards and beliefs.

Lucy's notebook:

Treating people as people is vital to success, as is having emotional intelligence. It is more important than anything.

Surrounding yourself with good people makes all the difference and that is from my years of experience working with good and bad people in a football club.

'That's the beauty of what he's done. He's surrounded himself with brilliant people.'

Jermaine Jenus - pundit and ex-player talking about Gareth Southgate, England manager, during the Euros 2020.

STRATEGY IN SUMMARY

KEY THINGS TO GET RIGHT

- Surround yourself with the right people – in life!
- Get your recruitment right first time and support them.
- Recruit for attitude.
- Surround yourself with winners.
- Always pick the best person irrespective of creed, race, gender.
- Beware of arrogance.
- Hire people with likeability.
- See people as a force.
- Use other people's skills to complement yours.
- Be really good at dealing with people.
- Don't stifle initiative.
- Make assessment part of your regular routine and make feedback instant.
- Deal quickly with bad behaviour.

5. JOBS

GET THE RIGHT PEOPLE DOING THE RIGHT THINGS

'My job is to help the boys to be the best players that they can be.'

Jurgen Klopp - football manager

JOBS: THE THEORY

Get the right people doing the right things.

Everyone working to a common goal

- Imagine your team building a house: everyone focused on the one vision. They all have different jobs and a range of different skills needed to make it happen – importantly there's a common goal.
- They all do their best and, depending on their experience and training, each person does it differently – different speeds, different quality and different results. All the effort goes into achieving the one overall objective – building the house.
- If one piece of the jigsaw isn't done properly it affects everyone else. It needs co-operation, planning and commitment.
- The three variables that we talk about in project management are quality, cost and time – if one of these changes, it impacts on at least one of the others.
- Applying this metaphor across all the activities of a football club is far more challenging, of course.
- Keep it simple – where the objectives are many or not so readily defined then it is difficult to focus energy on doing the right things.

Don't off – focus

Don't let anything disrupt the status-quo.

Stick to your principles, vision and goals at all times.

EVERY ACTIVITY SHOULD BE FOCUSED ON THE BIG PICTURE

- Everything that your team does should lead towards the achievement of your overall vision.
- In theory nothing should be done unless it goes towards building that house.
- Keep it simple – the more straight forward the goal the easier it will be to get people focused on achieving it.
- Can you answer these questions about your team or business area?
  - How much effort is wasted on non-productive activity?
  - How much time is lost through sickness?
  - How much time is wasted on rework – things that need to be done again?
  - How much time is lost through people not performing at their best?
  - How much time is lost on ineffective training?

- Wouldn't it be great if 100 per cent effort was performed at 100 per cent quality for 100 per cent of the time? How much more successful would you be?

Focus, focus, focus

If you chase two rabbits you will catch neither.

(Chinese proverb)

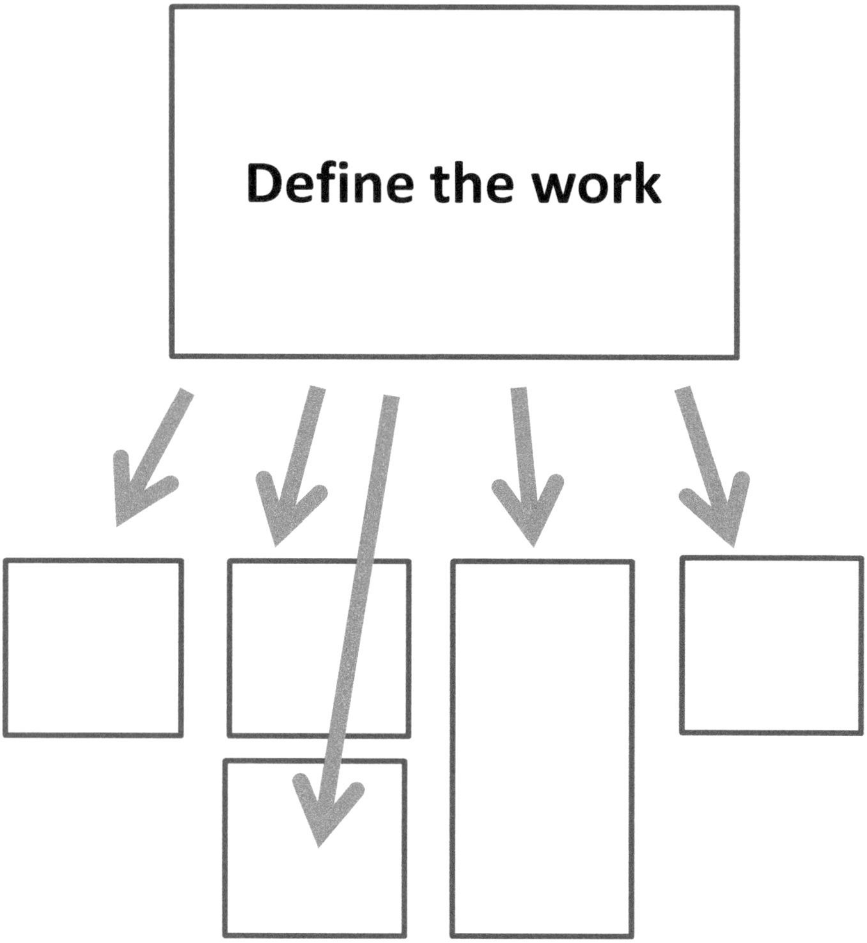

Break it down into jobs according to tasks that can be grouped together.

THEN ALLOCATE THE JOBS TO THE RIGHT PEOPLE.

BE CLEAR WHAT YOU EXPECT

- Peoples' roles need to be clear and well defined.
- When you're defining and planning work be absolutely clear what you want from people.
  - What needs to be done?
  - How will it be done?
  - How well will it be done?
  - Where will it be done?
  - By when will it be finished?
  - **Leave no room for doubt.**

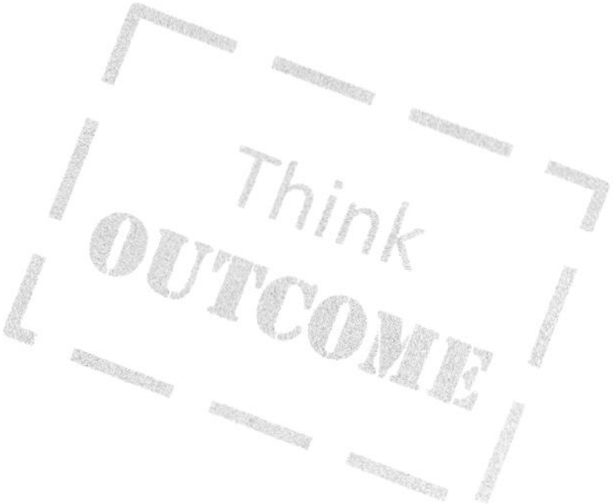

- Keep it simple – the more straight forward the goals the easier it will be to get people focused on achieving them.
- People like clarity – being clear about responsibilities and what's expected from them really helps from a leadership perspective.
- It helps make people feel good about themselves and people perform better when they feel good about themselves.

'We say all the time control the controllables and if you can focus and be the best that you can be at what you can control you give yourself an opportunity. If you start to cloud your mind with things which are beyond your control then you clog your mind up with things that can affect what you can control.'

Nigel Adkins - manager of Southampton FC before being promoted to the Premiership, April 2012

ATTENTION TO DETAIL

Attention to detail is important but it is worth remembering that too much detail can cause as many problems as not having enough.

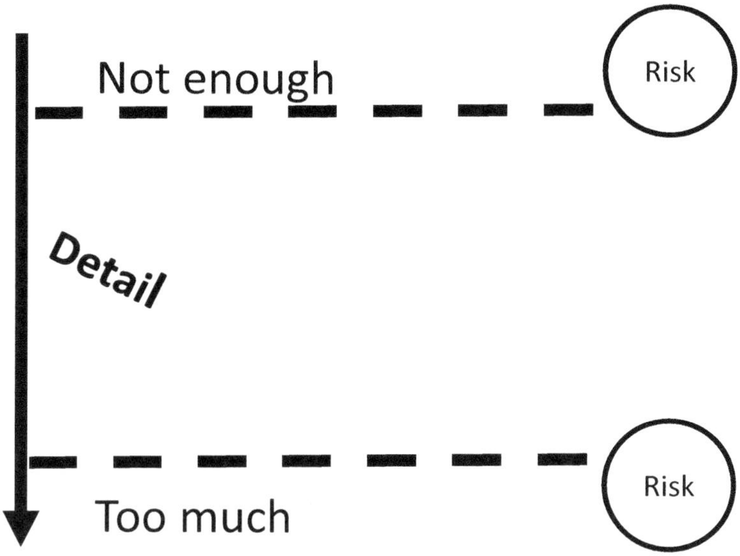

It depends, of course, on what we're talking about, but in general terms getting the right level of detail makes things easier to explain, understand and put into practice.

Keep things simple.

ROLE DEFINITIONS

- Roles must be 'complementary to' not 'in competition with' each other.

- Roles must be clearly defined so that job holders fully understand:
    - What they are expected to do and the boundaries within which they are expected to operate.
    - How well they are expected to perform and the rewards that they can expect in return.
    - The contribution they are making and how their job fits into the bigger picture.
    - Each role must contribute to the overall strategy, otherwise it is wasted effort.

- Sometimes boundaries have to overlap because you don't want things to fall through the gaps. Be clear to all involved who is responsible for what and when.

- Keep role definitions to the point and easy to understand.

- Keep role definitions up to date and review them in line with your regular reviews on performance to make sure nothing has changed.

'Football isn't instant coffee. You have to work at it. You must grow the bean, grind it.'

Ian Holloway - football manager

HOW DO YOU SPEND YOUR TIME?

Does your team focus their energy on the right things?

Use a simple pie chart to analyse what you spend your time doing. It doesn't have to be too detailed. A simple guesstimate will work.

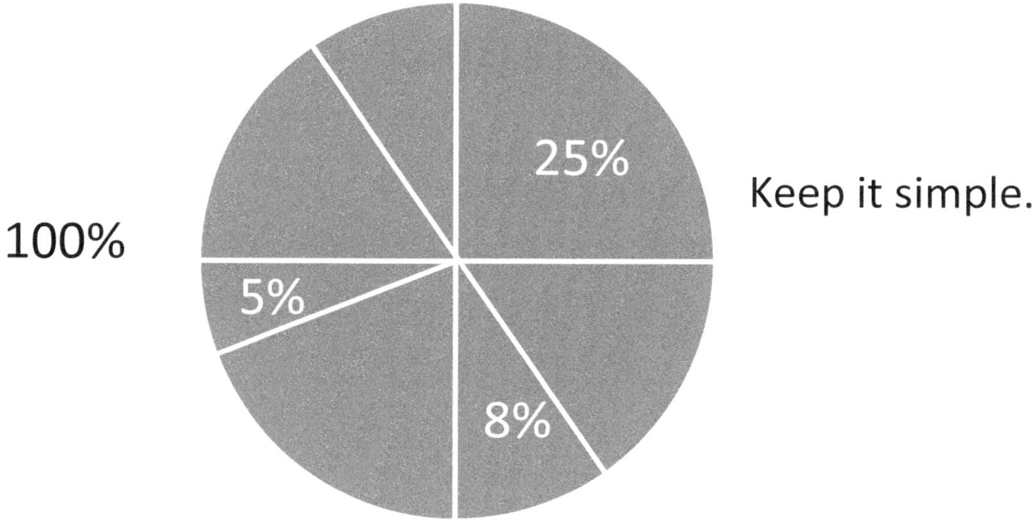

We all get into habits and daily routines and every now and again it is worth taking a step back and assessing whether we are spending our time on the right things.

Ask yourself – is it focused on the things that deliver the most benefits? Will it help us deliver our strategy?

Time wasted is time lost forever.

COMMITMENT: GET EVERYONE BOUGHT INTO THE VISION

- If people share the exact same dream then you have a very powerful team.
- If they are new and were not part of the visioning then sit down with them, get them to understand, get them to want it as much as you.
- Explain the benefits.
- They need to have an emotional attachment; they need to care about what happens.

Check and rationalise –

- Are they excited by it?
- Is it within reach? It doesn't have to be easy but it needs to feel achievable to keep the motivation.
- Are they passionate about it?
- **Do they care?**

Get everyone on board

Get your team believing in what you're doing and you have something very powerful.

Not just some of them. ***All*** *of them.*

CONTINUALLY TEACH YOUR STRATEGY AND APPROACH

As time goes by and people come and go, there will be members of your team who were not involved in any of the visioning or planning that now shapes your team. It's important therefore to continually keep people abreast of why you're doing what you're doing.

Remember the simple definition of strategy:
Knowing where you are today, knowing where you want to be tomorrow and having a plan to get there.

See section 3 for details of how to develop your strategy.

To be the very best, every single person in your team needs to understand what, why, how and when you are going to do things. And importantly the impact the person will have and the benefits of doing so.

'If the objective is the same and you all buy into it then you have a terrific ride ahead.'

Mike Phelan - assistant manager, Manchester United

THE PRINCIPLES OF GOOD PLANNING A REMINDER

See Strategy for more detail.

- A team's operational plans need to be aligned to the football club's strategic plans.
- Make a list of all the things that need to be done.
- Put them in some sort of order, remembering that some things might be dependent on others (e.g. if you are building a house the walls can't be built until the footings are in).
- Draw a timeline and put the actions that need to be taken under the appropriate dates.
- A trick is to start with the end date and work backwards (like planning a journey – what time do I want to get there? How long will it take? So what time do I need to leave?).
- Put in some milestones – things that can be achieved along the way to help target progress and a sense of getting to where you want to be.

Then:

- Sit back and assess whether your plan is realistic and achievable under your timescales.
- Have I missed anything?
- What would happen if ...?
- Plan, plan and plan again until you are happy.

Lucy's notebook:

Agree entirely with the start at the end and plan backwards. You have to know where you want to end up before you start the journey. Even if the journey changes direction for differing reasons you still need to start with direction.

'Good fortune is what happens when opportunity meets with planning.'

Thomas Edison – inventor

'Our goals can only be reached through a vehicle of a plan, in which we must fervently believe, and upon which we must vigorously act. There is no other route to success.'

Pablo Picasso – artist

A REMINDER: PRIORITISING YOUR TASKS

As shown in the Strategy section, it can be used for high-level planning as well as smaller routine tasks.

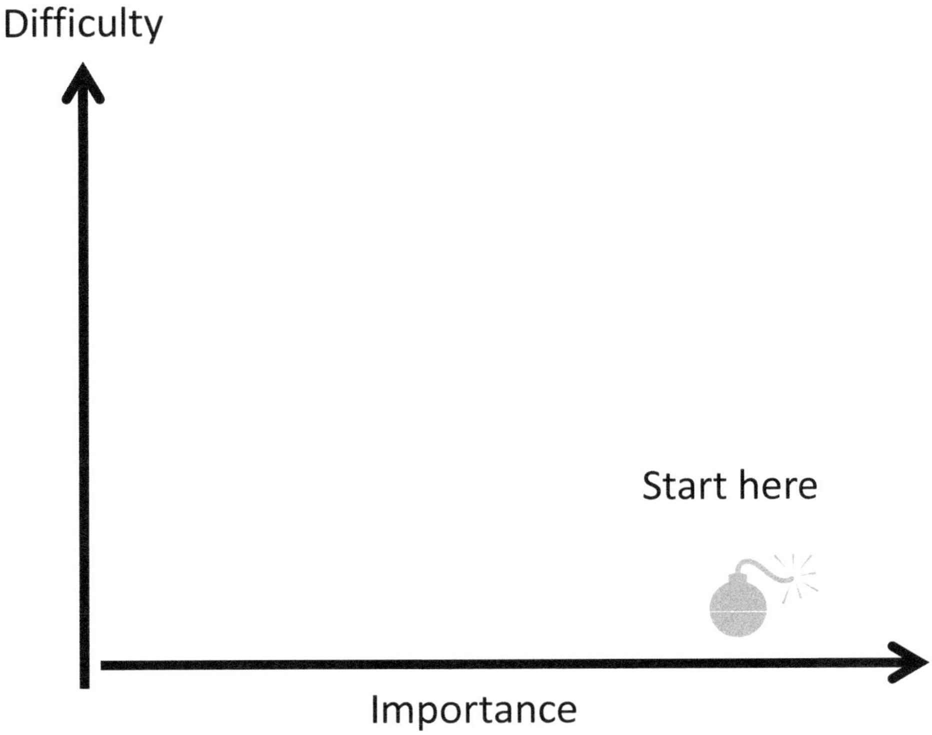

What's important?

What's easy to action?

Start with what's important and easy to action.

Get the quick wins.

PROCEDURES

The Oxford English Dictionary definition is: *A series of actions conducted in a certain order or manner; established or official way of doing something.*

- Procedures need to be well written:
  - Concise
  - Logical steps
  - Easy to read
  - Easy to understand.

- Procedures should:
  - Reflect best practice
  - Be followed without exception
  - Be part of training – especially induction.

- Keep them relevant.

- Continually review procedures to see if there is a better way of doing things.

- Keep them simple
  - The more complicated something is, the more chance there is of it going wrong and the more costly it will be to put right.

'The simpler I keep things, the better I play.'

Nancy Lopez - champion golfer

EFFORT

Nothing was ever achieved without hard work.

Talent alone is not enough – you'll know that the great Barcelona team as skilled as they were under Pep Guardiola, worked harder than anyone, always closing down the opposition when they didn't have the ball. They work and they work and they work. The same holds true for Pep's Man City team.

No one person is more important than the other – they just have different jobs and that includes the manager, coach, team captain ... whoever.

The ideal contribution is:

100 per cent effort

100 per cent quality

for 100 per cent of the time.

Note: work hard, play hard

Peak performance is not achieved through non-stop working.

You need a release.

You need sleep and rest.

You need enjoyment.

Have fun!

'Listen son. You've got to work harder. Simple as that. You've got to prove that you're good enough.'

Advice given to Sean Dyche by his father

CONTRIBUTION

The Oxford English Dictionary definition is: *that which is given in order to help achieve or provide something.*

- The key word in the definition is 'help' – contribution is about giving something towards the bigger picture along with other people.
- The sum of the parts equals the whole – be clear who needs to contribute what.
- Be specific about your expectations
  - What needs to be done?
  - How will it be done?
  - How well will it be done?
  - Where will it be done?
  - By when will it be finished?
- Get people working together in harmony to achieve the common goal.
- Encourage focus, minimise distraction and interruption.

There's an old story about a group of school children visiting NASA at the Kennedy Space Centre, Florida.

There was a guy there sweeping the floor. The teacher asked him what he did at the Space Centre and he replied:

'I help put people on the moon.'

How great is that? He believes that all his effort and hard work contribute to the vision – and of course he's right.

(Not sure whether it's a true story but it's still a great message.)

CONTRIBUTION: PERFORMANCE MANAGEMENT

- Performance Management in some organisations is just about setting targets and paying out bonuses.
- Performance Management should be about recognising people's strengths and weaknesses and helping them perform to their very best.
- Setting targets gives people something to strive for.
- Paying out bonuses (not necessarily cash) can be an extra inducement to achieve success.
- Be very careful to reward people fairly across the teams.
- Performance Management is People Management – nurture and grow your team and you will nurture and grow your operation.
- Make expectations and the method of measurement clear at the outset so that there is no room for subjectivity in the assessment of performance.
- Use the SMART technique for setting targets (see Strategy).
- Use KPI's for measuring performance (see this section).
- Just use common sense for paying out bonuses.

See *Measurement* later in this section.

Ideally...
Everyone should improve together with the same vision, strategy and objectives.
Is everyone in your team performing at their best?
Dedicated, focused, happy, determined – delivering?
How much time do you waste on things that slow you down, get in your way, stop you getting to where you want to be?

GET THE RIGHT TOOLS

This might seem obvious but some people just don't do it.

The Oxford English Dictionary definition is: *A thing used to help perform a job.*

- Get the right tools.
  - The right design to do the best job.
  - The right design for safety.
  - Keep them up to date.
  - Don't skimp on quality.
  - Keep them at optimum performance.
- Don't think of tools as just equipment and machinery. Tools are anything that you use to help you do a job e.g. mobile phone, goal-keeping gloves, computer software, training apparatus.
- Better tools = better performance, especially where there is a greater reliance on tools to do the job e.g. football boots.
- Buying the most expensive tools does not mean they are the best – it just means they are the most expensive.
- Science and technology is advancing all the time – keep abreast of developments.
- Giving people the right tools helps to make people feel valued. As we say throughout this handbook '*people perform better when they feel good about themselves*'.

Unusual to see these days - how about a peaked cap for goalkeepers to keep out the sun!
(Or keep out the glare of the floodlights if you're John Lukic playing against Glasgow Rangers.)

TRAINING

The Oxford English Dictionary definition is: *Teach a skill or type of behaviour through regular practice and instruction.*

- Training motivates and makes people feel valued.
- It helps with team bonding, especially when it's linked to a common goal.
- Have a plan for you, your team, your entire club.
- Make it specific to your needs – carry out a training needs analysis.
- Make it focused, and measure results.
- Assess performance and give constructive feedback.
- Monitor progress against the plan, and plan again.
- Take your training to a live environment only when you're happy with it.
- Give new people induction training. This is invaluable for improving performance and sends a strong message that training is important.
- Always train with a purpose.
- Link training to practice – learn something, practice it.
- Train, practice, train, practice, train, practice ...

'He wants to win, he wants to work, he wants to be the best.'

José Mourinho
- talking about Zlatan Ibrahimović

TRAINING: PRACTICE

The Oxford English Dictionary definition is: *Perform an activity or exercise a skill repeatedly or regularly in order to acquire, maintain, or improve proficiency in it.*

- When you learn a skill, you use your conscious brain to understand and apply that skill until through practice it becomes automatic and part of your subconscious (like driving a car).
- Your brain is essentially conditioned to perform that skill in a certain way through practice.
- Practice the right technique and you are conditioning yourself to succeed – practice the wrong technique and you are conditioning yourself to fail.
- Successful people practice more than unsuccessful people.
- Practice is not an optional exercise – make it disciplined, focused, targeted and work hard at it.
- Practice, practice, practice.

Train and practice at 100 per cent.

Put as much effort into your training and practice as you do into your performance.

Train hard.

Practice hard.

Success is directly linked to hard work and the quality of your training and practice.

TEAMWORK

The Oxford English Dictionary definition is:

- *two or more people working together*
- *a group of players forming one side in a competitive game or sport*
- Verb: *to come together to* ***achieve a common goal***

- Teamwork needs a special mention because the power of people pulling together epitomises a key rule of **●peoplemad** – *surround yourself with the right people.*
- Teams work well when they have:
  - A common objective
  - Complimentary skills
  - Camaraderie
  - The right people doing the right things
  - **Strong leaders.**
- People in a team have to be able to get on – they do not need to like each other, but it helps.
- **No one person is more important than the other** – they just have different jobs.
- Get rid of anyone who is not a team player or has a disruptive influence – you are better off without them.

Work hard at teamwork.

Teamwork doesn't just happen by itself.

It needs the right people.

It needs the right leadership.

'We don't always agree but once we make a decision we back each other 100%.'

Warren Gatland OBE - Wales Rugby Union manager

Lucy's notebook:

Brian McDermott was the manager of Leeds United during a particular volatile time ownership wise, but he was a real leader. He was softly spoken and quiet but had the greatest dead pan sense of humour ever. A lot of staff and players didn't know how to take him at first but he ended up with people eating out of his hand.

What did he do?

He took an interest in every single member of staff at the training ground starting off with those he knew would be perceived at the bottom of the pile of importance, but he knew they were in fact as important as anyone. The cleaners, the laundry staff, the kitchen staff, the receptionist, the academy staff etc. Everyone loved him and not for a good while had the club had a manager who made it his mission to get to know everyone. The effect was dramatic – even in that turbulent time people rallied with him and supported him and his vision. One of the best leaders of the club we had during my time at the club.

DEFINE YOUR TEAM(S)

- A football club will have a number of teams each with their own specific role all working together to achieve the club's objectives.
- You should know how your team fits into the overall operating model of your football club.
- It is very likely that the structure of the club will mean that you are in more than one team. For example, in the following diagram the people in team 11 are also in the larger teams 9, 4 and 1.
- It is important that they **know what is going on** in the larger structure.
- It is important that they are made to **feel part of what is going on** in the larger structure.
- You will need to think about how you align objectives, how you reward people and, importantly, how you communicate to make sure that all the teams work together and everyone is fully committed.

Keep an eye on motivation.

Is everyone in your team performing at their best?

Dedicated, focused, happy, determined and delivering?

DEFINE YOUR TEAM(S)

In a typical operating structure people can be part of a number of different teams In this example people in team 11 are also in the larger teams 9, 4 and 1.

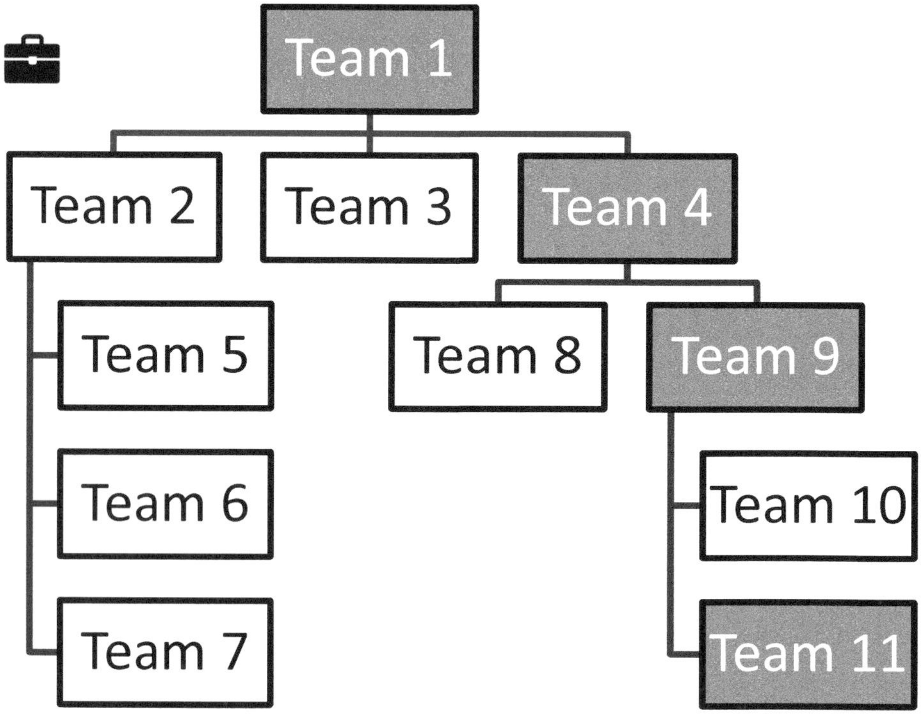

In this example, team 1 might be (say) the executive directors. Team 4 the operations executive, team 9 stadium management and team 11 security.

DISPARATE TEAMS NEED TO BE ALIGNED

Different Strategies? Goals? Plans? Policies? Guiding Principles?

ALL HEADING IN THE SAME DIRECTION

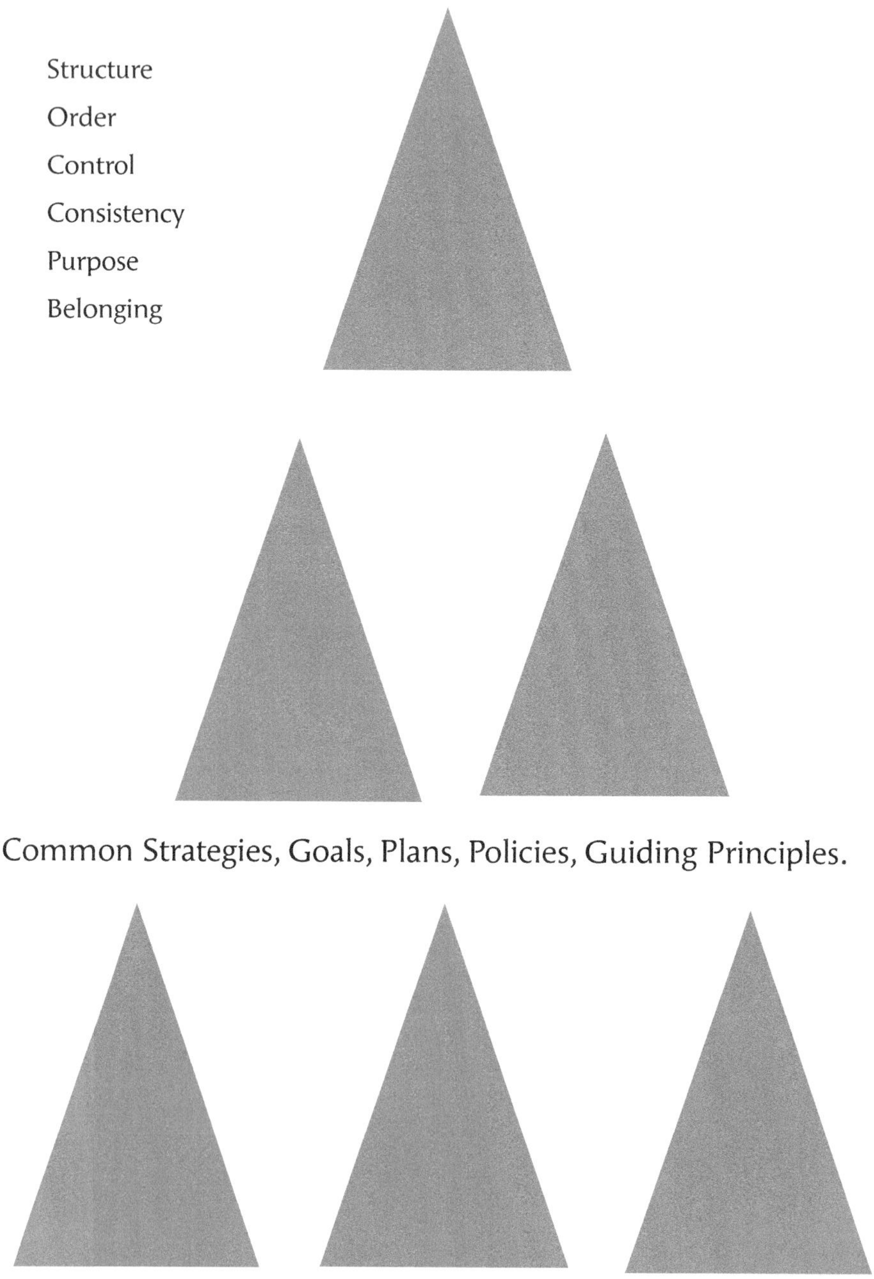

TEAMWORK: DELEGATION

The Oxford English Dictionary definition is: *A person sent or authorised to represent others; entrust a task or responsibility to others.*

- Delegation is an effective way to share workloads.
- Make sure the person being delegated to has the right capability to perform the task to the expected standard.
- Be clear about exactly what is being delegated.
- Agree scope, quality, outcome and timescales.
- You can delegate responsibility for something but you must remain accountable.
- Stay interested in the task and monitor progress.
- Give feedback on how well it was done.
- Delegation when done properly can be an effective part of someone's development programme.
- Offer help and advice where needed but allow people the chance to show what they can do for themselves.
- **Delegation of work to others is not one of the perks of being a boss. It is a tool to manage work effectively and it must be done properly and for the right reasons.**

Stay in control, monitor progress and give regular feedback.

What needs to be done?

How will it be done?

How well will it be done?

By when will it be finished?

It is not about giving people jobs you don't want to do yourself!

OBJECTIVES: SETTING TARGETS

- There are numerous models for setting and managing targets. SMART is one of the most well known, is as good as anything else and is simple to use.

SMART - make sure your targets are:

  - **S**pecific
  - **M**easurable
  - **A**chievable
  - **R**ealistic
  - **T**imely

- For paying out bonuses you should use common sense:
  - Keep them small relative to basic pay.
  - Make sure they drive the right behaviours.
- Always think about the outcome you want to achieve – will your targets make it happen?

'Pep lives every second of the day thinking about how to improve the side. Every second!'

Guillem Balague - writing about football coach Pep Guardiola

MEASUREMENT: KEY PERFORMANCE INDICATORS

- Think *high-level monitoring of what is going on in my area.*
- Improvement to all-round performance will require measurement and feedback on a number of different areas.
- KPIs are a set of quantifiable measures that gauge and compare the performance of an organisation in terms of meeting strategic and operational goals.
- Think of KPIs as indicators for different aspects of performance like a dashboard on a motor car.
- The word 'key' is important – just focus on a few areas.
- Limit them to those factors that are essential to the football club reaching its goals.
- Keep everyone's attention focused on achieving the same KPIs.
- These should be continually reviewed in line with performance to encourage new behaviours and activity.

Teams need a strong work ethic.

Make hard work a value for you and your team.

'This is one of our beliefs.'

MEASUREMENT: ACHIEVEMENT OF OBJECTIVES

Also see Strategy.

- The definition of performance as per the Encarta English Dictionary is: *The way in which somebody does a job, judged by its effectiveness.*
- In order to measure the effectiveness of a performance there has to have been a level of expectation laid down at the start – your set of targets and objectives.
- Define what success looks like.
- Naturally, the more specific the objectives, the easier it is to assess whether or not they have been achieved.
- How did you expect to perform? How well did you do?
- You, your team and your club should all have a plan of action to improve performance over time. These performance plans drive performance based on the vision, strategy and objectives.

Know what's important and measure it.
Continually measure what's important.
Especially the emotional well-being of your team.

SIMPLE TRAFFIC LIGHT SCORING SYSTEM

Green	Amber	Red
1	2	3
No attention needed	Needs attention	Needs urgent attention
Low priority	Medium priority	High priority
Strong performance	Average performance	Weak performance
Low risk	Medium risk	High Risk

The traffic light system is a quick and easy way to look at what needs doing and where you should focus your efforts. Detailed scoring systems with a greater range of values have their place, but they sometimes over complicate something which can often be quite simple. If it needs attention it needs attention.

Keep it simple: use coloured pens/highlighters or score 1, 2, 3.

You can use this system to assess most things, including the personal performance of yourself and the people you coach.

Lucy's notebook:

A lot of academies now will use this system when doing self-assessment activities with regards to the EPPP audit. It is so effective and gives focus and the ability to concentrate efforts in the correct areas.*

In terms of being a player, however, a lot of coaches work with players trying to improve their weaknesses rather than maximise strengths. By the time players get to scholar age, they should be marketing themselves in such a way that they are maximising what they are good at rather than working constantly on weaknesses. Even the best players in the world have weaknesses, but all we talk about is their strengths. Some coaches are too busy telling anyone who will listen what young players can't do rather than what they can. When I have review meetings with young players, I tell them they are self employed for their football career. If they are performing well then the club will benefit, but they are constantly earning their next contract wherever that may be.

*** Elite Player Performance Plan: A long-term strategy with the aim of developing more and better home-grown players. An initiative following consultation between the Premier League, football clubs and representatives of the Football League, the FA and other key stakeholders.**

HIGH-LEVEL FINANCIAL PLANNING

It is recognised that financial planning is critical in the running of a football club and that there are huge variances from country to country, league to league and club to club in the way that accounting practices are managed and controlled. The reason we cover the basics here is to ensure that leaders with little accounting experience understand the need for control, and to make sure their finances are working effectively for them.

- The main areas to consider are:
  - The overall impact on the profit-and-loss account.
  - The need to manage the cash flow – the timing of money coming in and money going out.
- Your budget: the whole point of budgeting is to give an idea of what you expect to receive (income) and spend (costs).
- A simple spreadsheet will often suffice for a high-level financial plan.
- If you are planning for a project then align the budget to the timeline of the project – and beyond if you want to keep a record of related income and costs that continue after the project has gone live.
- Income due to be generated as a result of the project should be planned and recorded separately to the running of the project.
- Use 'what if' scenarios to plan. What if this happens? What if I do this?
- Think about the *OUTCOME* that you want for *all* your decisions.

OVERARCHING FINANCIAL CONTROL

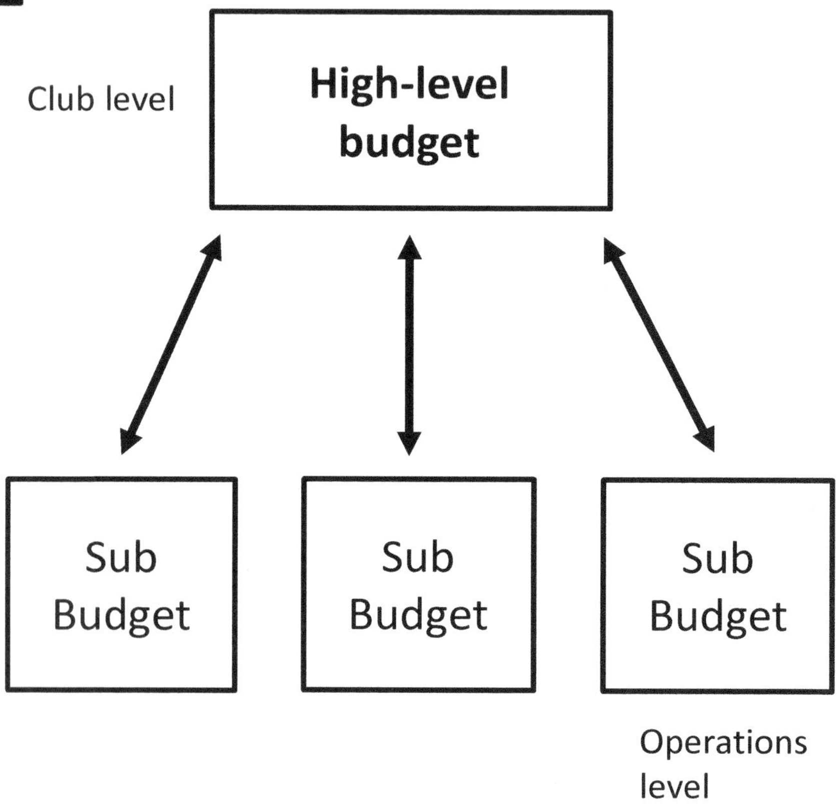

As with strategy, there should be one overarching budget at club level and the different playing and non-playing teams have their own budgets that add up to the overall total.

The important point is that ALL sections of the football club know what they have to work with.

HIGH-LEVEL FINANCIAL MONITORING

There are a lot of budget holders who do not know how well they are doing until they speak to their accountant. This is high risk and can end in tears.

It is important to find a way of knowing your figures ideally on a daily basis (even if they are only ball park) and have a system for projecting forward so you know how well your area will fair in the future.

If you're running a business area at a football club make sure you have a good relationship with your finance team. They are worth their weight in gold. They are experts in their field, use their skills to complement yours (see PEOPLE). They will prepare the right information for you which can help with critical informed decisions on how to run your part of the business.

You need to understand the financial consequences of every decision before you make them.

Why not keep your own 'back of a fag packet' notes on what you are going to get in and what you are going to spend – it will help you keep on top of things.

Football clubs actually have conflicting objectives. Running a business is generally about making a profit. Running a football club is about winning trophies. The cost of making a football club successful rarely allows you to run the club as a profitable business because the assets you need (i.e. players) tend to be an overpriced commodity. That's why the wealthier clubs tend to win all the trophies (with the odd exception).

RECOGNITION AND REWARD

The Oxford English Dictionary definition is: *A thing given in recognition of service, effort or achievement.*

- Reward can take many forms – usually cash, but never forget gifts, time off and, importantly, praise.
- Recognition for an achievement is very motivational.

- **Think carefully about how people are given recognition**
    - **if it is done properly it can motivate the rest of the team – *I want that.***
    - **If it is done badly it can demotivate the rest of the team – *what about me?***

- Remember people perform better when they feel good about themselves and being fairly rewarded is key (see **Leadership**).
- To be 'fairly rewarded' consideration needs to be given to the job in hand, how well it is being performed and how much other people are being paid as well.
- Get the balance right between incentives and basic pay.
- If you are paying a salary for someone to do a good job then a bonus should be exceptional – when someone has gone the extra mile.
- If a bonus is linked to a targeted performance then this should still be small relative to salary (see *Risks*).

- **Make sure incentives drive the right behaviours.**

RECOGNITION AND REWARD: RISKS

- Where people's livelihood depends on being successful, they are likely to take risks when things aren't going well to make sure that they stay in a job.
- Bonuses should only form a small percentage of the total package to avoid desperate measures if targets are not likely to be achieved.
- Be very careful what you incentivise. For example there is a huge difference between increasing market share and trying to get profitable market share.
- Think about team incentives to encourage everyone working for each other instead of against each other.
- How about a striker who is incentivised to score goals? Will he/she pass to another player in a better position. Probably not unless he/she is incentivised for assists as well.
- Know your subject, learn from the past. Think risk.
- Reward the right behaviours.

Make sure rewards are fair and are seen to be fair.

And remember sincere words of thanks go a very long way.

LEADERSHIP TIPS

- Even if you have the right people, it is wasted effort if you have them doing the wrong things.
- Think about the strategy – is everything focused on achieving your aims?
- How much effort is wasted?
- Give people the right training – avoid continual sheep dipping (giving the same training to everyone).
- Give people the right tools.
- You can delegate work but you can't delegate accountability.
- Always check the objectives to see if a job is being done properly or worth being done at all: 'what is it we are trying to achieve?'
- Align the development of your people to the development of your football club.
- Don't cut training budgets when times are hard. Never sacrifice the future.
- Keep things simple.

'One of sport's most vital lessons is that greatness is about remarkable individuals ... but it is about getting a remarkable amount of help along the way.'

Matthew Syed - international table tennis player and author

JOBS IN SUMMARY

KEY THINGS TO GET RIGHT

- Get the right people doing the right things.
- Focus on the strategy and plan.
- Learn how to delegate.
- Be clear what you want:
  - what, how and how well it will be done
  - by when it will be finished.
- Make processes effective and efficient.
- Target 100 per cent effort, 100 per cent quality for 100 per cent of the time.
- Train, practice, train, practice, train, practice ...
- Work hard at teamwork.
- Have a common goal.
- Set SMART targets and objectives.
- Make rewards fair and be seen to be fair.

6. ENVIRONMENT

Create an environment that breeds success.

'A football is the best toy ever invented. It brings with it hours and hours of pleasure.'

Sir Bobby Charlton

ENVIRONMENT: THE THEORY

People perform better when they feel good about themselves, so creating the right conditions will help them to work at their best.

This is about the general environment and much more than just the physical location where the activity is taking place.

This is as much about culture, atmosphere and rules as it is about having a coffee machine and a potted plant on your desk.

If you've ever seen a successful team with 'something special' then this is a big part of what made them superior and gave them the edge.

If you've got highly capable people doing the right things then when you create the right conditions that allow them to flourish you've got yourself something very special.

Put the right infrastructure in place, give people the right guidance and support and then allow them to grow and perform at their very best.

Think about every single part of your football club and everyone involved, including the fans. **Especially the fans.**

Where are we working? Does it help us get the best results? The pitch, office, gymnasium, retail store, running track, class room, training pitch ... is the lighting right, the equipment, the temperature? All conducive to delivering the very best results?

Whether it's about trying to sell merchandise or training to be the next League champions, the principles are exactly the same.

'I always thought that Anfield was a place more beautiful than heaven.'

John Aldridge - Liverpool footballer

Lucy's notebook:

At Leeds, for years the training ground looked good from the outside but it became tired and unloved by the owners. The recent owners have looked at it and made it into an environment that will help players and staff succeed and it has paid off.

> ***'The possibility of a European Super League in years to come makes Gillingham a prime location for a club to play in this competition, with it's proximity to the Channel tunnel and to Europe.'***
>
> **Paul Scally – Gillingham chairman, 2000**

Ironically, 21 years after that tongue-in-cheek comment from Paul, the proposed ESL failed at the first hurdle. Mainly due to a backlash from fans and media, with the wealthy club owners being accused of being greedy and not caring about or understanding grass-roots football.

CULTURE

Culture is the glue that binds everything together. This helps to create the 'je ne sais quoi' that gives a team the edge.

If you've got highly capable people doing the right things then when you create the right conditions that allow them to flourish and perform at their best, you've got yourself something very special. And a piece of advice if you're ever involved in the takeover of a football club – respect the old culture. If it needs changing then create a new one that everyone feels part of, one that they themselves have helped create. It takes time, of course, but that's part of getting it right.

Whilst it's mainly the people who make the culture, the physical environment plays a huge part as well. It's no coincidence that the City of Sheffield Athletic Club have the best coaches and state-of-the-art facilities and that Olympic Gold medallist Jessica Ennis-Hill just happens to comes from Sheffield. A great athlete who had the capability to be Olympic Champion wherever she was born, but the local environment helped her to develop her talents.

Of course, schools have a big part to play in a youngster's development. Yorkshire and England cricketer Joe Root went to the same school as Jessica, and Whitchurch High School in Cardiff has a reputation for producing top sports people, including Gareth Bale, Sam Warburton and Geraint Thomas.

Top facilities and importantly top coaches.

'You can only get a result out there if you've got total togetherness and total belief in each other.'

Graeme Souness - European Cup winner with Liverpool in 1978, 1981, 1984

'Any boy that's born within a 60 kilometres radius of here is showered with Athletico balloons and gifts; maternity wards are plastered in red and white. This football club becomes part of our identity from the second we're born.'

Jon Solaun - U16 head coach, Athletico Bilbao

'The post match party was important, and the venue was crucial, because many of the senior staff at Barcelona feel that the real golden moment is when the full FC Barcelona family is together – staff, players, directors plus assorted parents, girlfriends, wives, children and special guests – celebrating a year's hard work.'

Graham Hunter - from his book *Barca - The Making of the Best Team in the World*

'The 2003-04 team had everything. English players, foreign players. Physical players, technical players. A coach who knew his tactics perfectly even though they were simple: 4-4-2.'

Robert Pires – footballer, talking about the unbeaten Arsenal team

PEOPLE PERFORM BETTER WHEN THEY FEEL GOOD ABOUT THEMSELVES

People feel good about themselves when they:

- are treated with respect
- enjoy what they are doing
- know the rules and boundaries within which they operate
- know the level of performance that's expected of them
- believe in what they are being asked to do
- have the right skills, experience and knowledge for the job in hand
- are fairly rewarded for their activity and behaviour
- can see their contribution to the big picture
- feel that they are making a difference
- have a sense of belonging
- have certainty about their future
- like the people with whom they have to live, work and deal
- are surrounded by other people who feel good about themselves
- **are successful at what they do.**

This theme is embedded throughout the **●peoplemad model** *and is mentioned here because the environment is critical. Great leadership is what really makes it happen, which of course is key to getting the culture right.*

ENJOYMENT

The Oxford English Dictionary definition is: *The state or process of taking pleasure in something.*

(See 'sense of humour' in section 4.)

- Laughter is an enjoyable experience – it raises spirits and makes people feel good about themselves.
- Being able to laugh at things releases tension.
- Humour is a big part of team camaraderie.
- CAUTION:
    - Team camaraderie often involves 'mickey taking'; there is a limit to what is acceptable and it must not be cruel and divisive.
    - Work must be taken seriously and humour must not detract from the job at hand.
    - Always respect your colleagues, their workloads and their personal circumstances.
- You need to be able to laugh at yourself – it helps with team spirit.
- Work hard, play hard, have fun.
- Celebrate success.

'If you go out and play football to enjoy it you are going to play a lot better and get better results.'

Gareth Bale – international football player

GUIDING PRINCIPLES

- Have some guiding principles on expected behaviours (a *code of conduct* is similar but implies a set of rules rather than a set of values) (see Rules: discipline).

The Oxford English Dictionary definition:

- Values: *principles or standards of behaviour.*
- Morals: *principles of right or wrong.*

- Values and morals are beliefs about behaviour and what you perceive to be the difference between right and wrong.
- If different people in your team have different values/morals, this is likely to cause conflict.
- Naturally people feel strongly about their values/morals, and might not be prepared to change – which means the related behaviour will continue.
- The best teams have shared values:
    - Agree them together.
    - Keep them simple.
    - Get buy in and ownership from everyone.
- Stick to your principles – stay strong when they are tested.

'It's one thing putting core values up in a presentation, it's another thing living by them every day. And they can't just be mine and Nicky's values, they have to be everyone's. If you want to be a successful group you have to have a set of values you all adhere to and believe in.'

Danny Cowley - manager Huddersfield Town FC

SOME IMPORTANT POINTS

- Guiding principles are not a 'nice to have', they play a very important role in improving the performance of your team and football club.
- Be very careful about your wording and interpretation of the meaning. If you say 'the customer is always right' then your policies and processes need to reflect just that; for example, customers services, complaints, returns policy.
- Make them sincere. 'We trust and respect each other' are fine words but they have to be meant and again need to be reflected in your policies and processes; for example, HR manuals, code of conduct, disciplinary policy.
- Design your guiding principles to drive the right behaviours.
- Importantly, your principles need to be live and demonstrated across the club through behaviour.
- **It starts at the top – your leaders lead through their actions and words and these MUST reflect your guiding principles.**
- Make them visible – put them on posters, talk about them, be proud of them. Let everyone know, including your customers.

Think about how you deal with other people.
Assess how well you do it.
Ask yourself if you can do it better.
How you deal with other people will determine how other people deal with you.

'My job is not only coaching, it is transmitting values, which is something much more important.'

Marcelo Bielsa - head coach Leeds United

CONTROLS

You must have a controls. You need governance, risk management, standards, rules and policies telling people this is the way we do things around here. They need to be clear and simple; they don't have to be heavy handed but people need to work in a controlled environment. Naturally, if you work in the Nuclear Power industry your needs are going to be different to (say) working in a florists but the principles are the same. There are lots of risks at every level of a football club. Do you know what they are? It starts at the very top. Your legal structure and operating structures need to be right for your size of club (see Structure). You need to be absolutely clear who is responsible for running the business and who makes sure it doesn't take unnecessary risk – very often they are the same person, which in itself is a risk. As employers and employees we want to be happy that we are protected from risk. Controls give a feeling of security and certainty, as well as being a critical function of the day to day operation of the business.

The Head of Audit at British Airways used to remind people about the law of entropy – everything falls into dis-array unless checked. That's because controls are taken for granted. We forget to check that they're working; we don't have time, we get complacent because nothing has gone wrong. It's only when there's a scare that people worry about them, like the Heartbleed computer virus a few years ago that's made thousands of people change their passwords. Did you know that worldwide the cyber crime market generates more revenue for the criminals than the drug-trafficking market?

The right controls are a benefit not a burden.
They make good things happen and stop bad things from happening.

One of the biggest worries for most businesses is fraud.

In a well run operation there are usually back up controls so for things to go badly wrong more than one control has to be breached. That's why collusion between two or more people is difficult to stop.

When I ran the Audit team we had a tip off by the Police that a fraud ring was targeting our bank. We were told we had been infiltrated by a security guard, an IT specialist and a senior accounts clerk – giving access to buildings, computer systems, customer accounts and bank accounts.

Now, as far as collusion is concerned, this is a very potent cocktail of people. We put a small team together, worked around the clock and set up specific controls and reports to check for any abnormal activity ... and we waited, and waited ... and waited. Nothing happened.

Very pleased with ourselves, we reported back to the CEO and the main Board on all the possible ways that the fraud team could get money out of the system and all the extra controls that we'd put in place to prevent it from happening. We then realised that this report was dynamite if it got into the wrong hands. It was effectively a manual telling any would-be fraudster how to rob the bank. So after all our hard work, the report, all the files and reams and reams of working papers were destroyed.

At least that's what we told the Board.

Where there's money there's fraud – always be alert.

Treat the problem not the symptoms.

Make sure you understand the difference because symptoms come back.

Get to the root cause and stop it happening.

GOVERNANCE

The Oxford English Dictionary definition is: *The action or manner of governing; conducting the policy or affairs; control or influence.*

Football has the ability to make level-headed businessmen take risks they wouldn't ordinarily take in their normal line of business. Football fan emotion and business objectivity just don't sit comfortably together, which is why clubs need to make sure they have the right level of governance to stop passionate chairmen and directors taking risks in search of glory.

- Keep governance (the management of policies, standards, controls) completely separate from operational activity.
- Give governance and operational roles to different people e.g. keep the chairman and chief executive officer as separate roles:
  - The CEO runs the operation on a day-to-day basis.
  - The chairman has responsibility to shareholders/members to make sure the CEO and his executive team don't take undue risks.
- Non-executive directors have a responsibility to ensure that no one, including the chairman, takes undue risk.
- If you are on the Board, it is your responsibility to know what is going on in your football club. Stay very close to your accountants and auditors.

Leeds United's demise in the early part of this century was caused by financial recklessness and a lack of governance. The chairman Peter Ridsdale was both chairman and CEO; different roles with completely different objectives.

RISK MANAGEMENT

Risk

Create a risk management culture:

- Speak openly about risks and actions taken.
- Create a process to manage them.
- Keep it simple.

- The risks associated with taking any action should always be assessed.
- For most things in life we do it automatically.
- For projects and large-scale change, risk assessment should be a conscious effort and form part of your project management discipline.
- The level of mitigating action will be determined by how much risk you are prepared to take.
- Risks need to be assessed and managed on a continual basis not as a one-off event.
- What could go wrong?
- What do we need to do to stop it going wrong?
- What would be the impact if it did go wrong?
- Think of the impact especially on people, time and cost.
- Take responsibility for managing the risks of your business – stay close to your staff and the finances. No shocks.

There will always be risk.

Accept it. It's part of life. The more you do and the more you push the boundaries, the more risks you are likely to encounter.

The trick is to identify the risks before you make decisions, understand the consequences and manage them.

MANAGING RISK IS A CONTINUAL PROCESS

Risk

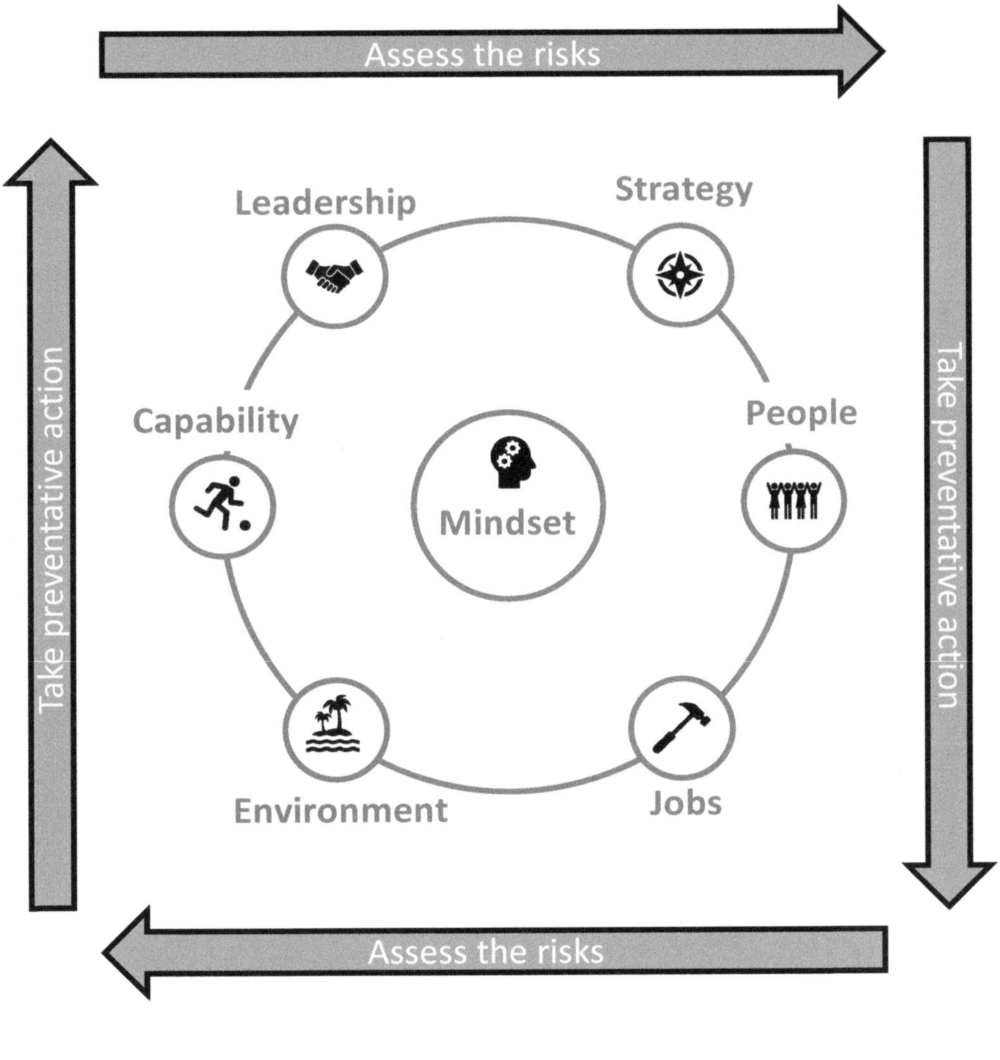

RISK: IMPACT ON OTHER PEOPLE

Risk

- Whenever you are making decisions and taking action it will invariably affect other people.
- People will be affected directly and indirectly, so make sure you fully understand the reach of your action(s), including the 'knock-on effect'.
- Think about the effect you are having on everyone's lives and think about the emotional impact.
- Think about the scale of the impact – fans, players, staff, customers, suppliers, media, other clubs, etc.
- Remember that you need other people to make things work.
- Think carefully about what you say and how you say it.
- This holds true for everyday life situations but is magnified in times of change.

And remember:
Risks never rest – they just change shape.

'I see my job as protecting it and improving it not changing it and ruining it.'

Andy Holt – chairman, Accrington Stanley

STANDARDS

The Oxford English Dictionary definition is: *A required or agreed level of quality or attainment.*

- At a personal level people have different standards.
- At a club level and team level agreed standards need to be in place so that everyone understands the level of quality they are expected to attain.
- Examples of standards might include:
  - dress
  - code of behaviour
  - customer service.
- Keep standards simple – easy to understand, easy to put in place and easy to monitor.
- Standards are important – they need to be part of your on-going training.
- Don't compromise – there is no point having standards if they are not enforced.
- Make them part of your culture.

Keep your standards high.
Make sure everyone knows the expected standards of performance and behaviours.
Don't compromise.

Lucy's notebook:

I remember Dave Hockaday coming into Leeds from non-league and mooting the idea to the first team that they should all wear the same type of trainers to away games. You can imagine how that went down with Championship players.

There needs to be standards but you need to know your audience.

'Results are the consequence of doing things well and having high standards, improving the detail of how we play.'

Gareth Southgate - England manager

PROCEDURES

The Oxford English Dictionary definition is: A *series of actions or steps towards achieving a particular end.*

- Procedures that define a set a processes by their very nature are a form of control – to make sure things are done properly i.e. to the required standard on a consistent basis.
- The best processes have controls built in:
  - to stop things happening
  - to warn you about things about to happen
  - to tell you when something has happened.
- In very simple terms the majority of controls fall into two categories:
  - Preventative: stopping things from going wrong.
  - Detective: identifying things that have or are about to go wrong.
- Control reports are a useful tool to monitor what's going on, what's likely to go wrong, what is going on.
- Exception reports do exactly that – report on things that look unusual, something that has happened that maybe looks out of kilter with the business-as-usual activity.

Don't use TLAs!

(Three Letter Acronyms)

RULES

The Oxford English Dictionary definition is: *Regulations or principles governing conduct or procedure within a particular area of activity.*

- At the highest level there is the need to comply with the rules and regulations laid down by the governing bodies. The penalties for non-compliance can be harsh so make sure somebody is given specific responsibility for managing it.
- Internally people need to know the regulations, especially those that apply within their area of activity **(don't forget the use of social media!)**.
- Enforce them (with no exceptions*).
- Make penalties clear.
- People are more likely to follow rules when they understand why they are there.
- Beware of using too many acronyms, they can cause confusion. If you do want to use them then make sure everyone knows what they mean.
- Make the rules relevant and not too bureaucratic.
- Continually review them to make sure they are still applicable.
- Keep them simple and sensible.

* If you allow exceptions, you immediately undermine the importance of your regulations and why you have them in the first place. You also open the door for other people to break the rules.

RULES: DISCIPLINE

The Oxford English Dictionary definition is: *The practice of training people to obey rules or a code of behaviour.*

- Have a code of conduct – this is how you are expected to behave.
- Make sure everyone understands the consequences for not complying with policies, rules, standards and procedures.
- Keep them simple, make them clear – no dubiety.
- Disciplinary procedures serve two purposes:
  - They act as a warning to prevent people breaking regulations.
  - They detail the punitive measures that will be taken if it happens.
- Always take action on breaches of discipline without exception.
- Discipline *must* be administered in line with the laid down policy and procedures.
- Disciplinary procedures must work and importantly be seen to work.
- Take action quickly – problems fester and get harder to deal with the longer they are left.
- When you have to punish someone you have not produced the right behaviours from your team. Could **you** have done anything better?

'In my early years at Aberdeen and Manchester United, I decided right away that in order to build trust and loyalty with the players, I had to give it to them first.'

Sir Alex Ferguson - football manager

Lucy's notebook:

Rules that are created by the whole team are important to the culture – a shared code of conduct is so strong, particularly in academies.

It facilitates buy-in from everyone and helps to create bonding and accountability.

'Sports teaches you character, it teaches you to play by the rules, it teaches you to know what it feels like to win and lose – it teaches you about life.'

Billie Jean King
– grand-slam tennis player

POLICY

The Oxford English Dictionary definition is: *A course or principle of action adopted or proposed by an organisation or individual.*

- There is a need to document and communicate the various policies that an organisation has in place.
- Policies need to be detailed because they have to cover every eventuality, especially the legal aspects to make sure there are no loopholes. These include:
  - Health and Safety
  - Human Resources
  - Disciplinary
  - Data Protection
  - IT Security.
- Continually review them to make sure they are still relevant.
- Keep them simple.
- Make them sensible – easy to read and understand.
- Only use legal jargon where absolutely necessary.
- Make them accessible to everyone who is entitled to see them – especially the people who are bound by them and/or have signed to say that they will comply.

Apply rules, policies, procedures with rigidity.
They are there for a reason.
If you fail to apply them properly then the system is compromised and they are not worth the paper they are written on.
This especially applies to disciplinary procedures.

COMMUNICATION

The Oxford English Dictionary definition is: *The sharing or exchanging of information or ideas.*

- See also 'meetings' – an important part of communication.
- Communication is two ways – sending and receiving.
- Communication should have a purpose – don't do it unless you are absolutely certain why you are doing it.
- If you are the sender it is your job to make sure it is properly received and understood – not the receiver.
- You can blame somebody for not listening but you can't blame someone for not hearing you.
- Before you say something think about the reaction you are trying to stimulate – what do you want the recipient to do? How do you want them to feel?
- Think about your words, think about the impact your communication will have. People are emotional creatures – what emotions will you stir up?
- Think about any language barriers. In a multi-cultural society not everyone will be fluent in the same languages.
- Make sure people 'get it' – received *and* understood.

> *For communication to be effective, it needs to be sent, received, understood,* ***and acted upon in the way the sender intended.***
> *This is exactly the same for verbal communication. Make sure it is clear, understood and acted upon as intended.*
> ***Always think about the consequences of what you put on social media.***

MEETINGS

The Oxford English Dictionary definition is: *An assembly of people for a purpose, especially for formal discussion.*

- Meetings are key to effective communication.
- **Don't have meetings just for the sake of it.**
- Whilst there can be many types of meetings in the main they fall into two categories:
  - Informal - quick catch up, chat, get things made clear.
  - Formal - serious issues that need serious attention.
- Be clear about the purpose of the meeting, think *outcome.*
- Only have the right people there (right people, right jobs).
- Some people feel they need to be at meetings just to know what's going on – *wrong,* unless that's the purpose of the meeting.
- Always appoint a chairman to run things and someone to take notes/ minutes – especially for formal meetings.
- For one-to-one meetings it is advisable to make notes. If it's a serious matter get both parties to agree them immediately afterwards.
- Have an agenda, stick to the time, keep discussions relevant.
- Meetings can be costly – see next page.

Make communication an agenda item.

After you've had a meeting make sure there is no ambiguity about who can say what to whom.

Agree who needs to know what and when.

Reiterate what needs to be kept confidential.

Meetings are costly when you consider operational down time, the time spent travelling and disruption to the working day.

As a discipline, work out the true cost of your meetings: the number of people X (number of hours at the meeting + travel time) X cost per hour + cost of travel for each person.

That figure excludes the cost of disrupting the daily routine for each person such as the other work that had to be put on hold while the meeting was taking place. It will scare you.

Use technology to save time and money, especially video and telephone conferencing.

And remember:

- Don't believe everything you read or hear.
- Check the credibility of your source.
- Effective communication doesn't just happen.
- **Always have a purpose to what you say and do.**
- Think about the impact of your words and actions.
    - Think what impact do I want?
    - What impact am I having?
- Before any communication think outcome?
    - What outcome do I want?
    - Will my words get the desired response/action?
- And Listen! Listen carefully to what people say and what they mean. They could be two different things.
- Also, remember that while you're talking you're not learning anything.

Communication is the lifeblood of an organisation.

Keep it healthy.

Keep it flowing.

People like to know what's going on.

*People **need** to know what's going on.*

COMMUNICATION: FEEDBACK

The Oxford English Dictionary definition is: *Information given in response to a person's performance of a task used as a basis for improvement.*

- Create a non-threatening, 'face-to-face' feedback culture.
- Feedback is good – that's how we learn.
- Feedback should not be taken as personal criticism.
- Feedback needs to be specific on process/behaviour.
- It should be supported by evidence – observation, facts and figures.
- Accepting feedback is difficult if you aren't used to it.
- Action needs to be agreed to improve performance as a result of the feedback.
- There is no such thing as negative feedback if it is delivered properly – it is positive in that ways to make improvements have been identified.
- Give training on giving and accepting feedback.
- Make feedback part of everyday life with your team.
- Catch people doing something well ... and tell them!

Critique the process not the person.

Talk about what could have worked better if it had been done differently.

If ... then, if ... then.

LOCATION, LOCATION, LOCATION

- Where you work, train, practice and do your day job has a direct impact on your performance.
- Make the physical working environment a pleasant place to be.
- People like space – cramped conditions aren't conducive to peak performance (especially after COVID 19).
- Have you got the right décor, lighting, temperature, windows, desks, chairs, equipment etc etc?
- Keep it clean and tidy – tidy space, tidy mind.
- Be mindful of Health and Safety regulations – they are there for a reason.
- When designing the environment think about:
  - The performance of the people using it.
  - How you want people to communicate (and recognise that sometimes people need privacy).

'Much of leadership is about extracting that extra five per cent of performance that individuals did not know they possessed.'

Sir Alex Ferguson - football manager

Lucy's notebook:

Covid has changed a lot of people's working practice. In my role at the Premier League, I switched to working from home very early on and couldn't make visits to club's academies that I had been used to taking. It was still effective with clubs and staff that I knew well and had been working with for years but for new clubs I found it really hard to forge relationships at the same speed as I would with face-to-face contact. Meetings without the non-verbal cues and behaviour you have when all in the same room are more difficult online. I think it has changed some people's way of working, some positively some negatively.

'I had two big problems with Becks, well he had with me! I used to go to bed at 9pm and wake up at 5am, he would stay up until 11pm and wake up at 8am, so essentially keeping me up from 9 till 11, then I was getting him up at 5am. So it just wasn't working at all. He is the cleanest person. He gets into his room, he lights candles, he puts pictures up, everything has to be perfect, it's been the same since he was 18. I just throw everything everywhere.'

Gary Neville about rooming with David Beckham

OBVIOUS BUT IMPORTANT QUESTIONS

- Do your training facilities get the best out of your players?
- Does it feel like home? You want your players to want to go there.
- What about your younger players? It needs to be fun. Yes they need to take training seriously, but they also need to enjoy the occasion.
- Is everywhere in good repair? People perform better when they feel good about themselves and being in pleasant surroundings every day certainly helps.
- Is your stadium the best it can be?
  - For your finances?
  - For your playing staff?
  - For your fans?

Remember your ground is a hallowed place for your supporters. It means much more than bricks, mortar and blades of grass. To fans it can be alive, with it's own beating heart.

'Montevideo's Centenario Stadium sighs with nostalgia for the glory days of Uruguayan soccer. Maracanã is still crying over Brazil's 1950 World Cup defeat.'

Edwardo Galeano - author

STRUCTURE

Understanding the big picture.

Structure is the organisational design and the operating structure within which people go about doing their daily work.

- The right structure is important for a number of reasons, including:
  - clarity of functions – what happens where
  - clarity of reporting lines – who reports to whom
  - clarity of accountabilities – who is responsible for what
  - the understanding of your role in the bigger picture
  - effective communication up, down and across the structure.
- This applies at every level – top down from boardroom to boot room.
- In your teams it is important to know who is responsible for what, who reports to whom and your role in the team.
- Have a look at how other football clubs are structured. It will vary, of course, depending on scale, from local town teams to inter-continental stretch like Manchester City.
- If you don't have a structure chart showing the different functions and who is responsible for what, try drawing one. It is a good exercise that will help you to think about the effectiveness and efficiency of the various operations within the club.

See also Teams in section 5.

Lucy's notebook:

Reporting lines are huge. At the bottom you need to know that your message and feedback is received at the top and doesn't just rely on a chance encounter with the 'boss'. A network of reporting lines must be efficient and effective. Managing up is one of the biggest issues faced with football managers nowadays. Sometimes faced with owners who have limited knowledge of football but high business acumen – the most unfortunate ones are the ones who think they have a high knowledge of football when in fact they don't.

The technical area can be a lonely place for managers for much of their career. It takes a lot of experience and knowledge to be able to handle decision making on match days and I'm not convinced it's fully appreciated by a lot of owners who don't always understand the game.

LEADERSHIP TIPS

- Lead by example and encourage others to do the same.
- Encourage communication, collaboration and co-operation.
- Continually review all policies and procedures to make sure they are appropriate and in line with changing conditions.
- Don't feel guilty about administering disciplinary action:
  - People shouldn't break the rules.
  - You can't make exceptions.
- Keep administration to an absolute minimum.
- Encourage focus, minimise distraction and interruption.
- Talk to people, ask questions, get involved.
- Make people feel part of what is going on.
- Most people like structure and order – link this to purpose and you have a strong foundation on which to build your team.
- People perform better when they feel good about themselves so it is important that they know their role and feel that they are contributing to the bigger picture.
- Celebrate success.

Create a positive feedback culture ***where people want feedback*** *to help them improve performance.*
I want to be the best I can be.
What can I do better?
Make positive feedback a habit.

ENVIRONMENT IN SUMMARY

KEY THINGS TO GET RIGHT

- Create an environment for success.
- Get the right location.
- Create the best conditions.
- Get the right operating structure.
- Create the right culture.
- Create some guiding principles and values.
- Make communication effective.
- Keep people informed.
- Use the right information.
- Communicate with a purpose.
- Create a positive feedback culture.
- Create the right controls, make them rigid.
- Keep an eye on risk.
- Keep your standards high.

7. CAPABILITY

Build capability for you and your team.

Trying to be the best and continually improving performance is one long journey – it never ends and as one destination comes into sight you should set your course for the next.

CAPABILITY: THE THEORY

This is about you and your team trying to be the best you can be.

Striving to build personal capability helps your own development and as a consequence naturally improves the overall performance of the team. And of course you need to lead by example. We can always learn new things – **•peoplemad** is about being the best and quite simply you won't be the best without working hard and doing absolutely everything you can to improve from where you are today.

> ***Matthew Syed, international table tennis champion, said in his book* Bounce*:***
> ***'The differences between expert performers and normal adults reflect a life-long persistence of deliberate effort to improve performance.'***

A life-long persistence of deliberate effort.

I too believe that success comes from hard work and a unique set of circumstances, which you can create for yourself.
Do you have a vision? Is it clear? Are you excited by it?
Are you passionate about it?

> ***'Everything I think, everything I do, everything I eat – will it make me go faster or will it make me go slower?'***
>
> **Adam Peaty - world-record breaking swimmer**

One of the issues for young adults is that they don't know what to do with their lives, so this model helps them with their career as well as giving them a grounding in sound leadership principles.

It will also help anyone coming to the end of their career or someone who might be looking for a change. As we all know, a career in football is not necessarily straightforward.

Have ambition and a plan be the best you can.

So what do I need to do to improve?
How do I get from my performance today to my better performance tomorrow?
What skills do I need?
You will be good at something if you:

- have the best coach/teacher/mentor
- learn the right technique
- work hard
- believe in yourself
- learn to be the best you can be
- practice, practice, practice
- don't give up.

And what about image? We've all got an image, how other people see us – is it how I want to be seen? What does my image need to be?
Remember people deal with people they like dealing with.

'If you've got to sweep a floor, make sure it's the best swept floor there is. If you can do something, do it right.'

Sean Dyche - manager, Burnley FC

What about my performance – how I perform on the day?

Whether it's playing the 18th hole at Augusta, a one-on-one with the 'keeper in a Champions League Final or coaching a class of students, the principles of peak performance are exactly the same.

Stay in the zone, don't reflect on mistakes, the missed putt, the missed penalty, forgetting your lines – and don't look too far ahead ... What if this? What if that?

Keep all your thoughts on the present, in the present.

The now is all there is. Get that right and the future takes care of itself.

'Focus, head down, blinkers on.'

Sir Nick Faldo - champion golfer

Success means different things to different people.

You need to understand what drives you, what makes you happy. How do you define your own success? We all want different things. Give yourself the advantage - do something better than everybody else.

Watch other people who already have that skill.

Do things. Read things. Learn things. Get interested in different things. Ask questions.

Be more interested in other people than you are in yourself.

Remember:

Improving performance starts with finding the right mindset.

I am, I can, I will.

TAKE OWNERSHIP OF YOUR CAREER

Whether working as part of a team or performing on your own, take ownership of your career and personal development.

- Clarify your vision.
- Devise your strategy.
- Carry out self-analysis – today versus tomorrow.
- Set some objectives.
- Develop a plan.
- Get the right attitude.
- Build your capability.
- Establish a support structure.
- Create the right image.
- Attain peak performance.

'Success comes from passion and a mixture of talent and motivation.'

A.V. Boas - football coach

There are lots of different jobs in the football industry. This section helps you to explore what really suits you, whatever your age, whatever your role is at the moment. Do you want a change? Has a change been forced upon you? Use this for yourself or to help other people who might want your advice.

YOUR CAREER LADDER

Using the career ladder analogy is a great way to put your career in perspective.

- How long is your ladder?
- Does it reach as high as you want it to?
- Do you know which rung you are on?
- How steep is it?
- How difficult is it to climb to the top?
- Is your ladder safe?
- Is someone 'footing' (securing) your ladder or trying to knock you off?
- **Are you on the right ladder?**

At some point you might want to change your job/ career.

There is nothing wrong with stepping off a higher rung of one ladder onto the lower rung of another if it is a longer ladder.

BE CAREFUL YOU DON'T FALL

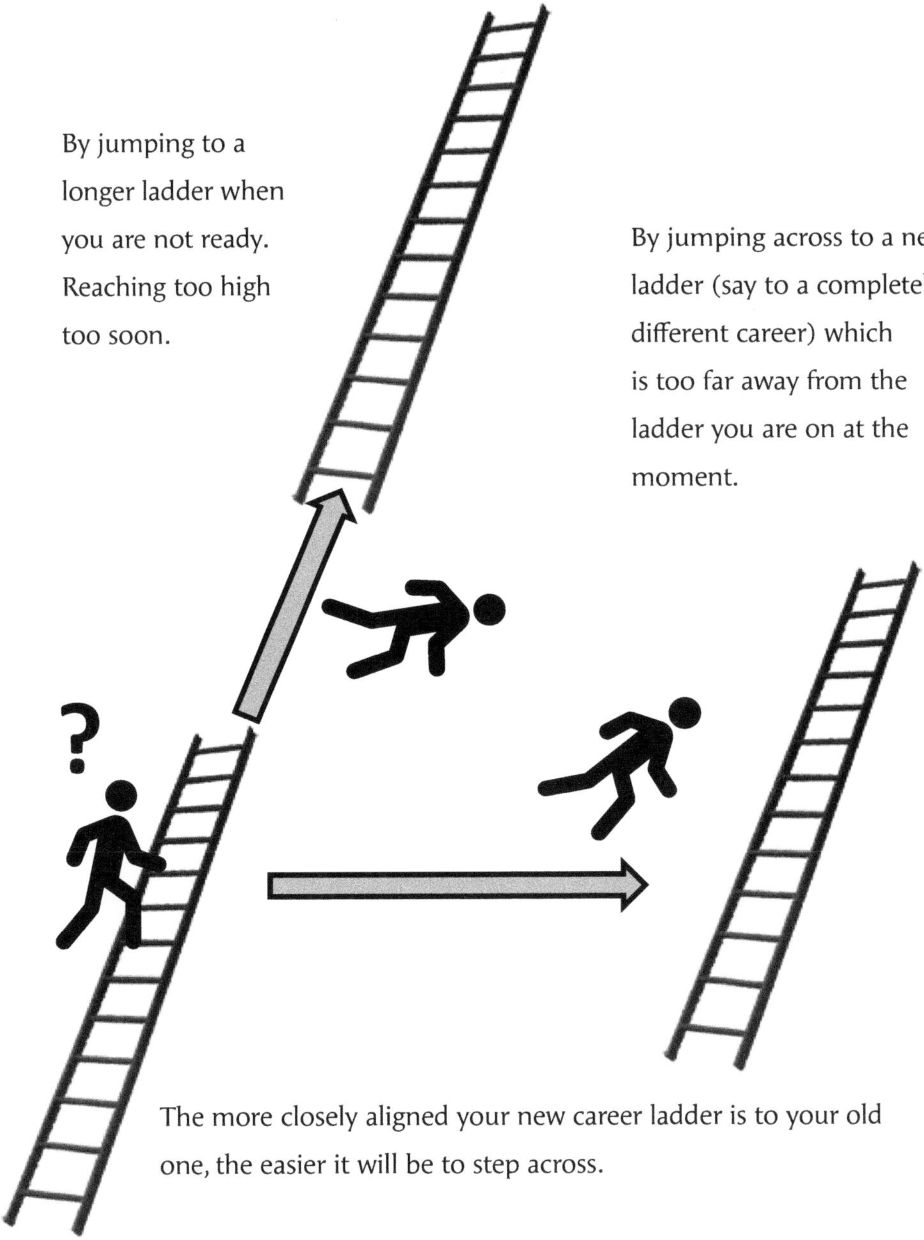

YOUR LIFE IS IN YOUR HANDS

You can achieve whatever you want providing you believe it's possible.

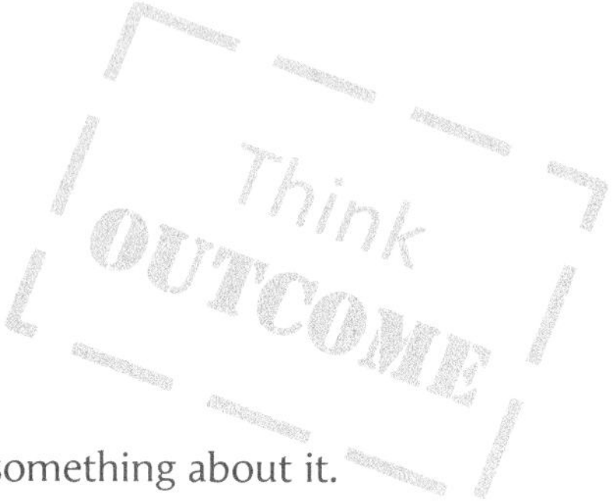

- Take ownership
  - Don't complain.
  - Don't make excuses.
  - Don't blame other people.
  - Don't put up barriers.
  - If things aren't working out do something about it.

- You need to get the best people on your side:
  - Believe in the ●**peoplemad** rules.
  - The only thing stopping you from achieving success is you – believe in yourself.

- It's your life – get on with it and make things happen.

What would you do if you knew you couldn't fail?
What would you do if you didn't care what people think?
Would you do things differently?

'I told mum one day "I'm going to play football for Anderlecht. It's going to happen soon..." I was six.'

Romelu Lukaku
– footballer, on achieving his dream

Lucy's notebook:

The biggest thing I had to learn was being bothered what people thought about me. Now, more than ever, I get extra attention because I'm commentating on TV – some negative but mostly positive fortunately. It is human nature to concentrate on the negative, but it is so important to move away from this.

Don't take criticism from someone you wouldn't take advice from.

It is actually empowering to not read negative thoughts about my TV performance on social media. The most important people are the ones who give you the work and the people closest to you who will tell you straight. This obviously applies to the positive messages too. In all performances you can never get too carried away with either success or failure.

Lucy's notebook:

There are certain quotes in Baz Luhrmann's Sunscreen *which I love.*

'The real troubles in your life

Are apt to be things that never crossed your worried mind

The kind that blindsides you at 4pm on some idle Tuesday

Do one thing every day that scares you

Don't waste your time on jealousy

Sometimes you're ahead, sometimes you're behind

The race is long and in the end, it's only with yourself

Whatever you do, don't congratulate yourself too much

Or berate yourself either

Your choices are half chance, so are everybody else's

Be careful whose advice you buy but be patient with those who supply it

Advice is a form of nostalgia, dispensing it is a way of fishing the past

From the disposal, wiping it off, painting over the ugly parts

And recycling it for more than it's worth.'

DEVELOP YOUR GAME PLAN

Create your vision.

Think it.
See it.
Want it.

- Aspire, desire, dream.
- Open your mind.
- Don't put restrictions on your thoughts.
- Believe you can do anything that's physically possible.
- Research it.
- Draw it, paint it, write it down.
- Give it as much detail as possible.
- Sleep on it.
- Close your eyes and paint it in your mind.

Check and rationalise:

- Are you passionate about it?
- Can you get excited by it?
- Is it within reach? It doesn't have to be easy but it needs to feel achievable to keep motivated.

DEVISE YOUR STRATEGY

Knowing where you are today:

- Carry out a review – a self-analysis (see next pages).
- Understand you and how you feel about things.
- Understand your life, your career and where you are today in as much detail as possible.
- Assess everything – including other people in your life.
- Be truthful to yourself as to the realistic position.
- The more honest and accurate the information the easier it will be to plan.

Knowing where you want to be tomorrow:

- Start with your vision.
- Take your thoughts and drawings and turn them into detailed descriptions of what the future looks like.
- Think of everything, especially the people you would like to get involved to help you.

Having a plan to get there:

- Plot how to move from today's position to the described vision – prioritise and plan.
- Be creative.
- Don't put up barriers.
- Get other people involved, especially those who will be working with you or impacted by your strategy.
- Get buy-in and support as early as possible.
- Assess the risks and put mitigating plans in place.

WHAT MOTIVATES YOU?

- Money?
- Enjoyment?
- Pride in the job?
- Helping others?
- Is your motivation intrinsic? e.g. feeling good.
- Is your motivation extrinsic? e.g. trophies and glory.
- Remember you'll be better at something if you enjoy doing it.

Picture your ideal day

- Travelling or based at home?
- Office based or out and about?
- Working alone or mixing with people?
- What do you see yourself doing when you wake up in the morning?

Over 35,000 people run in the London Marathon every year knowing that they can't all win. So they must be motivated by something other than winning. Raising money for charity, the fun, the sense of achievement?

When he reached number one in the world golf rankings, Rory McIlroy said his motivation was just to be better than everyone else. Brilliant.

What drives you? What excites you? What is important to you?

CARRY OUT SELF-ANALYSIS

- Describe how you see yourself today in as much detail as possible:
  - Give your own view.
  - Get a friend's view.
  - Get a relative's view.
- Describe how you see yourself tomorrow in as much detail as possible:
  - Be creative.
  - Be realistic.
  - Don't put up barriers.
- Carry out a gap analysis between the present and future state:
  - Where are the main differences?
  - Do you understand why?
  - Identify where you want to make changes.
  - Think about the risks of making the changes.
  - Think about the risks of not making the changes.
  - What are the positives?
  - What are the negatives?
- Prioritise your actions and create a plan.

'You are a long time retired. I don't want to be there when that happens and think "oh I wish I had done that better".'

James Milner - footballer

TODAY VERSUS TOMORROW
SOME EXAMPLE QUESTIONS

- What motivates you?
- What do you like about yourself?
- What do you dislike about yourself?
- What makes you happy?
- Anything you feel strongly about?
- What upsets you?
- What annoys you?
- Who inspires you?
- If you could change one thing?
- Unfulfilled dreams?
- What do you like doing?
- What do you think about?
- How do you spend your day?
- Are you an introvert or an extrovert?
- Are you a fashion leader or follower?
- What do you worry about?

You need ambition, something to aim for, something to get you excited about the future.

'I got up every day to beat Barry Sheene.'

Kenny Roberts - world-champion motorcyclist

TODAY VERSUS TOMORROW
SOME IDEAS

- Skills
- Knowledge
- Experience
- Good at?
- Bad at?
- Beliefs
- People
- Music
- Hobbies
- Emotions
- Fashion
- Friends
- Family
- Image
- Views
- Religion
- Home
- Work
- Travel
- Character
- Bad habits
- Food
- Fitness
- Charities
- Phobias
- Worries and concerns

'We cannot solve our problems with the same thinking that we used when we created them.'

Albert Einstein

'Stay hungry, keep motivated and give it all.'

Ada Hegerberg
- BBC Women's Footballer of the Year 2019

SET SOME PERSONAL OBJECTIVES

- You now have a vision and a strategy – objectives will give focus to make it happen.
- When you describe your vision then you need to attach some objectives that will make you achieve it.
- Keep them simple.
- Make sure they are the right ones and lead you down the right path.
- Describe them in such a way that there is no doubt when they are achieved.
- Set some short-term objectives – they will act as stepping stones and give a sense of achievement along the way.
- Get buy in – think about everyone who is impacted by your actions.
- Communicate progress.
- Celebrate success when they are achieved.

'Anyone that knows me, knows I like to try new challenges, new skills, I want to be learning all the time about different things. If I'm not good at something, I love the journey of getting better, learning the ins and outs of something.

It brings me a lot of joy being on that journey.'

Hector Bellerin - footballer, Arsenal FC

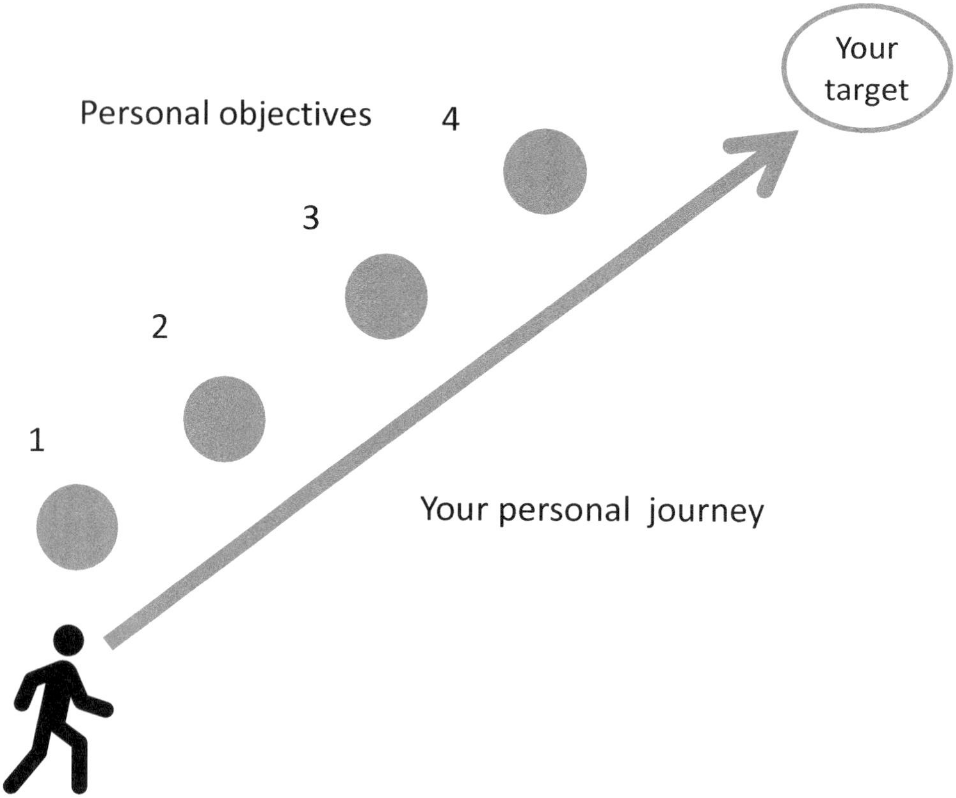

Have ambition and a plan.

Be the best you can.

DEVELOP YOUR PLAN

See Strategy for more detail.

Here is very brief summary:

- Make a list of all the things that need to be done.
- Put them in some sort of order remembering that some things might be dependent on others (e.g. if you are building a house the walls can't be built until the foundations are in).
- Draw a timeline and put the actions that need to be taken under the appropriate dates.
- A trick is to start with the end date and work backwards (like planning a journey – what time do I want to get there? How long will it take? So what time do I need to leave?).
- Put in some milestones – where you want to be by a certain point in time. This will help target progress and give a sense of continual achievement.
- Sit back and assess whether your plan is realistic and achievable under your timescales.
- Have I missed anything?
- What would happen if?
- Plan, plan and plan again until you are happy.

'I had to have the power of the mind and I had to be the fittest, and these are the two things that I applied diligently as a young man and still do.'

Arnold Palmer - champion golfer

DEVELOP YOUR COMPETENCIES

The Oxford English Dictionary definition is: *Having the necessary ability or knowledge to do something successfully.*

- *The trick is in how this ability and knowledge is applied.*
  - Attitude: *Settled way of thinking or feeling*
  - Talent: *Natural aptitude or skill.*
  - Skill: *The ability to do something well.*
  - Knowledge: *Information and skills acquired through experience and education.*

- Competence is not finite – your attitude, talent, skill and knowledge are all areas that can be continually improved through effort.
- Experience comes from doing things. It is not about age. Get out there, do things, read things, meet people and learn new things.

'Take control of your life off the pitch to empower your performance on it. There are no limits to what you can achieve within sport and beyond.'

Mark Roberts - former professional footballer and athlete mentor for the FLE (League Football Education)

... AND WHAT ABOUT THESE SKILLS?

Listening:

Do you listen to understand?

Or do you listen to respond?

You'll learn a lot more by listening to understand.

You're not learning anything when you're talking.

Understanding other people:

How they think.

How they behave.

The impact they have on you.

The impact you have on them.

Making decisions:

Options? Pros? Cons? Relativity? Facts? Timing? Outcome? Consequences? Benefits? Costs? Risks? Impact?

The greater your knowledge and experience the better your decisions will be.

Life is about choices.

Success is about making the right choices.

Making great notes:

If you want to make great notes, make them thinking you're going to have to explain them to someone else.

> ***'I always questioned myself in the best of times, even when I was World number 1.' 'What can I improve? What do I need to change?'***
>
> **Roger Federer - grand-slam tennis player**

GET THE RIGHT ATTITUDE

- Be a winner:
  - Work hard.
  - Be the vision; be that person today.
  - Display leadership:
    - Listen.
    - Inspire.
    - Make decisions.
    - Show respect.
- Be confident:
  - Solid eye contact.
  - Of course I can.
    - I am the star of my own show.
    - I am taking this space.
- Be in control:
  - Rise above everything.
    - Choose what you want to believe and hear.
  - Feel interested not threatened.
    - 'What makes you say that?'
  - Stay in adult state.
    - Be the parent not the child.
  - Influence don't be influenced.
    - Be the conductor of your orchestra.

'Talent will get you into the dressing room. How you behave determines how long you remain there.'

Txiki Begiristain – director of football

POSITIVE ATTITUDE

- Success comes from 100 per cent belief.
- The body does what it is told by the brain.
- 70,000 thoughts a day (so they say) – don't waste them.
- Don't talk about failure.
- Don't even think about failure.
- Believe, make it happen.
- Moaning adds no value whatsoever.
- If you don't like it do something about it.
- Don't worry about things you can do nothing about.
- Don't worry about people who do not affect your world.
- Negativity is draining.
- Look forward – get excited.

'I was 12 when I started and 34 before I achieved my dream, that should give people hope.'

Dame Kelly Holmes - Olympic champion

A positive attitude is everything.

Because you can make things happen.

Negativity is draining and has no value whatsoever.

'I judge my players for their intentions, not for the result.'

Pep Guardiola - football manager

Lucy's notebook:

I think that self talk is a really positive way of dealing with difficult situations. It also gets you used to situations where it is just you, no one else and only you who can do whatever is necessary. This I apply to my commentary. Although I get help from others it is just me who decides what to say in the heat of the moment so therefore you should trust and train your inner voice to support and encourage but, above all, trust your ability and capabilities.

'When I was a kid, I was told I wasn't good enough. But, I loved the game.

So I ignored the doubters and kept practicing. Eventually I got better and stronger.

So find what you love, keep at it and be as good as you can be.'

Alex Morgan –
footballer, United States women

DEVELOP A WINNING MENTALITY

See also Mindset and People

The Oxford English Dictionary definition is:

- *Winner: a person or thing that wins.*
- *Mentality: characteristic way of thinking.*

- Winning people have winning ways – they know what's needed to be a winner.
- Winners inspire other people to be winners.
- Winners are positive people – they don't think about failure.
- Winners usually have high energy levels and a desire to get things done.
- Winners who have tasted success want more of it.
- Winners hate losing – '*show me a good loser and I'll show you a loser*'.
- Be a winner, **surround yourself with winners.**

Never give up.
Believe in yourself.
Keep your vision alive.
Remember why you're doing it.
Keep working hard.

'I'm happy I chose to go down that route of working unbelievably hard.'

Roger Federer - grand-slam tennis player

WINNING MENTALITY: MAKING ACTIONS COUNT

- Try to make *all* your actions count.
- Think about why you are doing something.
- Always aim to have a positive OUTCOME.
- If it's worth doing it's worth doing properly.
- What OUTCOME do you want?
- Does it move you nearer towards your goals?
- Often your desired OUTCOME will be determined by a series of actions; if one isn't carried out properly then this could affect the benefits of the others. They could even be completely wasted.
- Focus on them all – they all count.
- Concentrate to the end – be relentless.

In golf the last short putt is as important as the 250 yard drive off the tee. To be a good singer you need to hit every single note.

Footballers have to deliver the final pass. All the previous good passes count for nothing when there is a shot off-target, a missed penalty, a bad cross – wasted effort that makes all the previous actions wasted effort as well.

The best performers know how to complete the job properly – concentrate, focus on the task, deliver.

'Winning doesn't really matter as long as you win.'

Vinnie Jones – footballer and Hollywood star

STRENGTHEN YOUR ABILITY

- Develop your people skills:
  - How to manage other people.
  - How to manage yourself.
- Develop core skills:
  - Talent.
  - Technique.
  - Practice, practice, practice.
- Improve your knowledge:
  - Job in hand.
  - Competition.
  - Watch and learn from other people – find a role model.
- Get as much experience as you can:
  - Make it targeted, have a plan.
- Get your fitness levels up to the required standard:
  - Physical and mental.
- Build your communication skills:
  - Actively listen.
  - Get interested in people.
- Push the boundaries:
  - Stretch the comfort zone, try new things.

Work on all aspects of improving performance

Skill levels – ability.

Physical conditioning – preparing your body.

Psychological readiness – the right mind-set.

WORK HARD, PLAY HARD

- Peak performance is not achieved through non-stop working.
- You need rest and the right intake of food so that your energy levels are at their highest when you need them.
- It is important to have a release. If things aren't going well or you are working too hard and all you have in life is your work then it will affect your health.
- To avoid stress or depression you need other things to take your mind off your work. This can be anything – catching up with your favourite TV show or just taking time out to rest and reflect.
- Practice relaxation techniques such as yoga and meditation.
- Find a hobby or a sport that you enjoy doing for fun.
- **Caution** – Beware of continually finding your release in partying, drugs, alcohol and gambling! This will negatively affect your energy levels and even your mental health, making matters worse not better. Socialising is good but remember that to be the best at what you do, you will need to be refreshed and able to perform at your peak.

'Working hard for something we don't care about is called stress. Working hard for something we care about is called passion.'

Simon Sinek - author and motivational speaker.

ALSO PRACTICE YOUR THINKING SKILLS

Think **OUTCOME. Y+E=O.**

- How **you** deal with other people will determine the **outcome**. Take control.
- Decide how you want to think about the **event**.
- Decide what outcome you want.
- Consider your actions.
- Take the right steps to deliver your desired outcome.

Think **IMPACT**

- What impact am I making?
- Is it the desired impact?
- Link impact to outcome – what do I want to achieve? What impact do I want it to have?

Think **RELATIVITY**

- Look at *everything* relative to *everything else.*
- 'Being the best' is a relative statement. You will only be the winner if you are better than somebody else.
- To win, do everything you can to improve your capability and understand the capability of the competition.
- Always think about the relative importance of something before prioritising and taking action.

Think carefully about the impact before changing a decision. Changing your mind for the right reason is obviously OK but can be disruptive and hinder progress especially if people have already started to take action.

ESTABLISH A SUPPORT STRUCTURE

This is about the environment and the people you need to help you achieve your vision, such as mentors, coaches, managers, personal assistants, doctors, sport scientists, teachers, colleagues, friends, family, advisors etc.

- Surround yourself with the right people:
  - Right attitude:
    - 100 per cent commitment to the cause.
    - Belief in the vision.
  - Right ability:
    - Right skills.
    - Right knowledge.
    - Right experience.
  - Doing the right things:
    - All actions focused on the vision.
- Create the right environment to enhance your performance:
  - In training.
  - In work.
  - At home.

Get a leadership coach

Leadership is knowing how to get the best out of yourself and helping others do the same.

It makes sense to build your leadership skills.

It makes sense to get a coach to help you.

'No matter what accomplishments you make, somebody helped you.'

Althea Gibson - grand-slam tennis player

ATTAIN PEAK PERFORMANCE

This relates to performing 'on the day' from a single task to a complete performance which could take hours.

- Prepare properly beforehand. This will give you the right level of confidence to perform on the day.
- Visualise your performance, see great things happen.
- Do everything you can to feel good about yourself.
- Clear your mind – ready to think about the task in hand.
- Get rid of distraction and disruption.
- Stay focused – concentrate only on the performance.
- During the performance stay in the present:
  - Don't reflect on mistakes.
  - Don't look forward thinking what might happen.
- Stay within your comfort zone – don't try things you've not perfected in training.
- Nerves are OK, use them to fire up your performance.
- Stay positive – no negative thoughts whatsoever.
- Stay confident – 'of course I can'.
- When you are winning 'go for the kill'. Stay focused, don't get complacent, don't ease off. Don't think *victory*, think *performance*.
- Don't listen to negative comments from other people.
- Give 100 per cent effort and enjoy!

'I've had a lot of abuse and still scored my goals. I've zoned it out and carried on playing my game.'

Timo Werner - youngest player to make 200 appearances in the Bundesliga

Lucy's notebook:

I worked really hard as a player on my fitness, especially the last half as I got older. I found that if I was the fittest in the team this would give me the confidence to play well and know that when things got hard I could always fall back on my fitness to help me through the toughest of situations. When I was younger I relied too much on my natural talent and fitness. Not many women played football and I was one of the best on my team as a kid even though the rest were adults. I needed pushing by someone and given the correct advice. If I was young now I would be a much better player earlier just because of the opportunities available to female players as children. My only regret is that I didn't work as hard on my game until later on in my career.

'You play at the rhythm you train at. If you train badly, you play badly. If you work like a beast in training, you play the same way.'

Pep Guardiola – football manager

PEAK PERFORMANCE – MINDSET

Peak performance doesn't just happen.

It comes from preparation, hard work *and your attitude on the day.*

Stay in the now.

Peak performance needs the right mindset.

Don't look backwards or forwards thinking what if?

Focus on the process not the outcome.

Focus, stay in the 'now' and don't reflect on mistakes.

> ***'I just needed to stay focused and stay in the present and just really concentrate on what I was doing.'***
>
> **Rory McIlroy - champion golfer**

Here's a great example of the power of visualisation:

> ***'I don't know why but I have always asked the kit man what colour kit we are wearing, found out what colour the opponents are wearing and visualised scoring goals, or good things happening in the game. I do it before every game, get good thoughts, good moments happening in my head.'***
>
> **Wayne Rooney - footballer**

Learn a skill. Practice it. Embed it in your subconscious.

Practice the right things and practice them properly – otherwise you'll embed the wrong things.

Practice, practice, practice.

SOME IMPORTANT POINTS

- To prepare and perform at your very best you must:
  - Keep sight of your vision.
  - Stay positive – don't tolerate negativity.
  - Believe in your ability.
  - Continually stretch your comfort zone in training.
  - Stay within your comfort zone during performance.
  - Practice, practice, practice.
  - Reward success – treat yourself when you've done something well.
- Surround yourself with the right people – the people who will help and support you in achieving your vision.
- Don't tolerate the wrong people – they will spoil everything for you or at best slow you down.
- **Work hard, play hard**. See Work Ethic in section 4.

'Champions keep playing until they get it right.'

Billie Jean King - grand-slam tennis player

Start now.

Even if it's small steps.

Don't wait until tomorrow to start improving your performance.

CREATE THE RIGHT IMAGE

- In its simplest form, 'image' means how you are seen by other people.
- Everyone has an image.
- Do you know how other people see you?
- Is it how you'd like to be seen?
- Image covers everything:
    - overall look
    - behaviour
    - brand
    - clothes
    - website
    - social media
    - things you say
    - **people you mix with.**

- Choosing the right image can help improve performance by making you feel good about yourself.
- It can also help with your popularity – 'people like dealing with people they like dealing with'.

'It's really important for me to look good before a race. I definitely think if I feel I look good, it makes me feel more confident.'

Dame Jessica Ennis-Hill - Olympic champion

Think: Dress for the job you want not the one you've got. This is about mindset. Start now. Adopt the image, attitude and behaviour of the person you want to be.

PERSONAL LIFE

- Stick to the **●peoplemad** rules.
- Have ambition – look forward, get excited.
- Have a plan for what you want to achieve.
- You are who you mix with.
- You need to surround yourself with the right people – those with the right attitude.
- Watch and learn from other people – find a role model.
- Make sure you do the right jobs that give you the right experience for what you want to do as a career.
- Do the things that you enjoy doing – you will be good at them.
- You need to work in an environment that allows you to flourish.
- Display leadership qualities at all times.
- Take control – don't let other people control your life.
- Don't compromise your values – ever.
- Lose the wrong people – now. It's their loss not yours.
- **Caution** – Do not surround yourself with 'yes' people who just say what you want to hear.
- **Remember you represent your football club at all times.**
- **Think about your behaviour, think about the image of yourself and your club.**

'Everyone's dreams can come true if you just stick with it and work hard.'

Serena Williams - grand-slam tennis player

REMEMBER ...

- Everything revolves around you.
- You are in control of your thoughts and actions.
- You decide what you do, no one else.
- Other people affect your happiness and success – learn how to choose them, learn how to deal with them.
- You decide what you do with your life and your career, don't rely on other people to do it for you – other people have their own lives and careers to worry about.
- How you deal with other people will determine how other people deal with you.
- Take ownership
  - Don't make excuses.
  - Don't blame other people.
  - Don't put up barriers.
- Be self-aware
  - Think about what you do
  - Assess how well you do it
- If things aren't working out do something about it.
- Get the best people on your side.
- Get on with it and make things happen.

Build your people skills

Especially:

- influencing
- reasoning
- listening
- handling conflict
- explaining things.

'Achievement is largely the product of steadily raising one's level of aspiration and expectation.'

Jack Nicklaus - American golfer

Lucy's notebook:

Listening skills are important!

In my younger years I was desperate to 'get on' and sometimes listened to respond instead of listening to understand. I work really hard on the latter as I am excellent at the former! I find that listening and not being as eager and impatient has helped me in all my job roles.

Some of the best leaders I have encountered listened to people to understand.

'I would urge players to study, to learn a language, or take up a commercial course. It's going to help you. Don't just look at the play station.'

Edwin Van Der Sar – former player and CEO of AFC Ajax on the importance of professional development

CAPABILITY IN SUMMARY

KEY THINGS TO GET RIGHT

- Continually build capability to be the best you can be.
- Learn how to plan.
- Be clear what you want to achieve, focus on your goal.
- Be clear what you need to change.
- Don't restrict yourself.
- Work on all aspects of performance.
- Build your people skills.
- Find your true motivation.
- Make hard work one of your values.
- Learn to visualise.
- Know your competition.
- Enjoy what you do.

CAPABILITY IN SUMMARY

KEY THINGS TO GET RIGHT

- Develop a positive attitude.
- Practice, practice, practice.
- Be approachable.
- Start today.
- Never give up.
- Be great at making decisions.
- Build your support team.
- Understand your impact.
- Work on your performance, focus, stay in the now.
- Be effective, make all actions count.
- Create the right image.
- Live your brand.

8. LEADERSHIP

GET EVERYONE BEHAVING AS LEADERS

The whole book is essentially about leadership. This section focuses specifically on key leadership behaviours.

LEADERSHIP: THE THEORY

Leadership is as much about taking control of your life as it is about leading other people – stand up and be counted. You don't have to be a manager to display leadership qualities.

Take ownership of the actions of yourself and your team.

Do the right things, direct the actions of others to help achieve the vision.

Inspire others through your actions and words. Get people motivated to achieve the vision.

Give help, advice, encouragement: **make people feel good about themselves.** Support them with an open hand. Don't stifle them.

Picture the future, create ambition, share the excitement.

You can be that person. You don't have to be in charge of people to do those things.

Leadership is about being accountable and taking ownership.
Have a purpose to what you say and do – what outcome do you want?

Think carefully about your leadership style. Your actions affect other people, think about what you say and how you say it and the impact you are having on other people's lives.

Changing your own behaviour is only half of the equation. Great leaders change the behaviour of others.

Also be approachable.

You need to know what's going on in your area of responsibility - the last thing you want is for colleagues to be frightened of telling you things. And be honest with people, even if the message is a difficult one. If it's not appropriate to say anything then you tell them it's not appropriate.

Lucy's notebook:

I have had many leaders who I have worked for and with. Brian McDermott would make you feel like a million dollars and had this innate ability to get everyone with him, primarily through his kindness, empathy, sense of humour and people skills.

'It's really important how you say things because people won't necessarily remember what words you used but they'll remember how you made them feel.'

Brian McDermott – football player, manager, coach

'And in the end there is a price that's more important than the titles. Titles are just numbers. It's what you give or leave to the player to work with, and there's no one player, there's no one team, that cannot admit all of them were better persons or better players, and that is the best trophy you can get as a manager.'

Pep Guardiola talking about Marcelo Bielsa's impact as a coach

'For me, it wasn't about whether the coach was the best technically or tactically, but how he made you feel.'

Andy Farrell OBE – international rugby coach

'The chefs at Brentford have a purpose. Get the players ready for the games as best you can. Do everything to help the club get promoted. You may be the first people the players see every morning so set the atmosphere. Help pick players up after a poor result. They are given responsibility and more importantly are made to feel a big part of the team.'

Fraser Franks - footballer, talking about Brentford FC. head coach Thomas Frank including all the staff in a photograph celebrating winning Manager of the Month.

We can all be leaders. Help people do their jobs better and this in turn will help you do your job better.

In November 2005 I went to watch Leeds play Crewe Alexandra at Gresty Road in the Championship – the second tier of English football. Leeds had not long been relegated and were managed by Kevin Blackwell – his first attempt at being a manager. There's mistake number one by the Leeds United board – a huge club with ambitions to get back into the Premier League and they appointed somebody who had never done the job before.

Anyway, we were awful and lost 1-0. I was on my way home listening to Radio Leeds and Kevin came on and said how badly they had played, he criticised the players and said he was going to let them know that he wouldn't tolerate it. Some of them wouldn't be playing for the club again. He distanced himself from the performance.

I'm angry, I've told the players, I won't tolerate it.

On the same evening Chelsea also lost 1-0, to Real Betis, and José Mourinho, the Chelsea manager, came on the radio.

We have no defence or argument for it.

We are a great team, we have got to get back to our standards.

We have to look at ourselves to work out what didn't work and try to solve it.

He took ownership, he was accountable, he used the word 'we'.

Kevin blamed the players, José didn't blame anyone.

Kevin distanced himself, José took ownership.

A few years later Kevin was sacked by Bury and unfortunately still hadn't learnt, publicly calling his players 'garbage'.

José Mourinho has his faults, of course, but nevertheless is one of the most successful football leaders in the world.

BE ACCOUNTABLE

The Oxford English Dictionary definition is: *Required or expected to justify actions or decisions.*

The **●peoplemad** definition is: *taking ownership!*

- You don't have to be in charge of something to display leadership qualities.
- Take ownership
  - Don't complain.
  - Don't make excuses.
  - Don't blame other people.
  - Don't put up barriers.
- If things aren't working out do something about it.

'If you are selfish, if you think about yourself and you don't care about the club, don't care about the image, don't care about the fans then we are in big trouble.'

José Mourinho - when Chelsea manager

The ancient Romans had a tradition. Whenever one of their engineers constructed an arch, as the capstone was hoisted into place, the engineer assumed accountability for his work in the most profound way possible: he stood under the arch.

An essential quality of leadership is being accountable and taking responsibility for your own actions and the actions of your team.

> ***'I honestly don't believe I should be here answering questions on behalf of the players. They should be here answering questions on why their performances were so poor. To be honest with you, I don't think it's my responsibility at this stage to answer for a performance as bad as that.'***
>
> **Stuart Pearce - after his England team's poor display in the European U21 Championship, June 2013**

As a football manager you are responsible for picking the team, training them, coaching them on tactics and motivating them. If the players don't deliver, how can you distance yourself from their performance?

Stuart's contract was not renewed by the FA.
An unfortunate example.

Live your brand.

Remember you represent your club and team at all times.

Think about your image.

Think about your team's image.

Make sure they are aligned to the brand values of your football club.

How you look and how you behave.

A NOTE ON COMPETENCE

The Oxford English Dictionary definition is: *Having the necessary ability or knowledge to do something successfully.*

- The trick is in how this ability and knowledge is applied.
  - Attitude: *Settled way of thinking or feeling.*
  - Talent: *Natural aptitude or skill.*
  - Skill: *The ability to do something well.*
  - Knowledge: *Information and skills acquired through experience and education.*

- Great leaders have a learning mind-set.
- To be a leader, there is often a natural expectancy from other people that you know what you're doing.
- You can't be expected to be good at everything and have infinite knowledge. Be honest.
- The trick is using what you do know to act decisively and take the initiative.
- If you don't have sufficient knowledge to make a decision then find it.
- Competence is not finite – your attitude, talent, skill and knowledge are all areas that can be continually improved through effort and **especially decision making – successful leadership depends on it.**

'Stay at the leading edge of the game. I may grow older, but the players are still young. For their sake, I must never stand still.'

Brendan Rodgers - football manager

MAKE THE RIGHT DECISIONS

- Effective decision making is about achieving the desired outcome.
- Be absolutely clear about the outcome you want.
- Weigh up the options, pros, cons, consequences, benefits, costs, risks and impact.
- Don't restrict your thinking; think *what would happen if?*
- Get all the right information before making a decision.
- Is it accurate? Is it timely (up to date)?
- If you don't have the right information, find it.
- It is impossible to be an expert on everything – be honest with yourself about how much you know.
- Use the knowledge and experience of other people.
- Your *gut feel* saves time and is usually right. This only works if you have the right knowledge and experience. Test it. Make sure it works for you.
- Always think about the impact of your decisions before making them.
- Don't make decisions based on emotion. Take away emotion and make a rational well-informed decision.
- If you are still uncertain and you have done all the necessary thinking, analysis and testing then console yourself with the fact that both/all options could work and are likely to achieve a similar outcome.

'Big managers are never afraid to make big decisions.'

John Terry – football player and coach talking about José Mourinho

FORESIGHT

The Oxford English Dictionary definition is: *The ability to anticipate future events or requirements.*

- The ability to anticipate future events comes with knowledge and experience – it is not a gift or a supernatural power.
- Get to know your subject matter, your industry, other clubs, your own football club, your surroundings and importantly your people.
- You will get better at this if you continually look ahead and plan the future and then check back to see what happened.
- Compare your expectations with the actual results.
- Practice. Try short-term and long-term forecasts.
- Watch and listen to the media – read reports.
- Get up to date expert knowledge in your field – become the expert yourself.
- Foresight is a skill. Learn to be good at it.

'I never make predictions, and I never will.'

Paul Gascoigne - footballer

VISION

See also Strategy in section 3.

The Oxford English Dictionary definition is: *the ability to think about or plan the future with imagination or wisdom; a mental image of what the future will or could be like.*

- As a leader, people will look to you for direction. You need a clear vision of what you are trying to achieve in order to point people in the right direction.
    - Be passionate about it.
    - Get excited by it.
    - Get other people excited by it.
- Continually check and ask yourself:
    - Why are we doing it?
    - Is it within reach? It doesn't have to be easy but it needs to feel achievable to keep people motivated.

'A characteristic of the successful soccer teams I have worked with is a simplicity and clarity of message. Good coaches agree with their teams that this is where we want to go, this is how we are going to do it, and this is the role that each of us has to play.'

Bill Beswick - elite international sports coach and leader in the field of applied sport psychology

GIVE DIRECTION

The Oxford English Dictionary definition is: *The action of directing or managing instructions on how to reach a destination or about how to do something.*

- Encourage communication, collaboration and co-operation.
- Strong leadership is about getting the best results from the other people involved.
- A strong team will have many people with leadership qualities – the trick will be to channel those qualities for the good of the team.
- Don't confuse strong leadership with forcing your will on others – this will just cause resentment.
- Get skilled at making the right decisions at the right time.
- Get to know your subject matter, especially your people.
- Do not be afraid of making difficult decisions.

Fly high to keep an eye on what's going on.
Fly low and zoom in on what's important.
Help, support, sort out the issues.
Soar back out again.

'The captain is basically the messenger of the manager. I always think that when a relationship between a captain and a manager is strong, it makes the team stronger and it makes the manager stronger.'

Arsene Wenger - football manager

CO-OPERATION

The Oxford English Dictionary definition is: *Work together towards the same end; help someone or comply with their requests.*

- The act of co-operating is fundamental to teamwork, building relationships and working with other people.
- Co-operation is not:
  - 'giving in' to someone
  - doing something because you've been told to
  - a sign of weakness.
- Co-operation is:
  - doing something that helps both/all parties
  - a quick way of getting something done
  - a sign of strength.
- Collaborate – helping someone else with their performance can help you with yours – a *win-win* situation.

Co-operation the Graeme Souness way:

Kennedy played it long. Souness called for it short again. Kennedy went long again, prompting Souness this time to march up to him.
'I couldn't see you, Graeme,' said Kennedy.
Souness wound back an arm and punched him flat in the face.
'Can you see me know?' he asked.

Extract from Quiet Genius, Bob Paisley's biography by Ian Herbert.

Lucy's notebook:

I have worked on a lot of tournaments in different countries for the BBC and Channel 4 over the years, including broadcasting in vast places like China & Canada. The team would consist of 'talent' (comms, pundits and presenters) and also the real talent (camera operators, sound/vision, producers, directors etc) and it is always a logistical nightmare because of the complexity of what we have to do. It always works well because we have a real leader at the heart of it.

It is such a difficult job and a little like herding cats, but the key is communication, making decisions quickly and importantly being able to adapt to everchanging situations.

'I've never scored a goal in my life without getting a pass from someone else.'

Abby Wambach – women's USA international footballer, member of the National Soccer Hall of Fame

INSPIRE OTHERS

The Oxford English Dictionary definition is: *Fill with the urge or ability to do or feel something – create a feeling in a person.*

- Be able to inspire others **through your actions and words.**
- People watch what you do.
- People comment on what you do.
- People copy what you do.
- Do you know how other people see you?
- Is it how you'd like to be seen?
- Think of the impact of your actions on other people, directly and indirectly.
- Get to know your subject matter, especially your people.
- Live and breathe the guiding principles.
- Set an example – be the example.

Always treat people with dignity and respect.
Because it's the right thing to do.

'It's easy to go out and put performances in like that when you've got somebody leading you like that.'

Ben Foster WBA - talking about manager Darren Moore after beating Manchester Utd at Old Trafford

LEND SUPPORT

The Oxford English Dictionary definition is: *Give assistance, encouragement, approval, emotional help – be actively interested.*

- Be there for people in times of need.
- **Treat everyone with empathy, respect and dignity.**
- Give frequent and honest feedback on performance.

- Think about your own behaviour:
  - Leadership is not about bossing people around.
  - Do you ask people to do something for you or do you tell them? Courtesy is to ask.
  - Do you say 'I' or 'we'? – you are part of a team it should always be 'we'.
  - Do you thank people for doing things? Just because it is someone's job to do something you should still show your appreciation.

- Politeness is a strength and manners are very important.
- Remember – a key part of leadership is about making people feel good about themselves.
- Surround yourself with the right people.

Be approachable.

You don't want people scared of telling you things.

People deal with people they like dealing with.

Lucy's notebook:

My role at Leeds involved supporting the coaching and other disciplinary staff to develop young players. Welfare is a massive part of this, it is very difficult to produce a player from a young person who is unhappy or uncertain about life and where they fit within life. That doesn't mean you simplify their life and solve all their issues for them. It means you identify any issues then work with the player to handle and have the tools to deal with issues. From a staff point of view, I banged on and on to coaches that you have to walk in the shoes of all players before judging their reactions. Why are they behaving like they do? What language do I use with them, including my body language? Do I explain my decisions and give feedback so they can process where I am coming from?

I remember a lad being upset due to being 'dropped' for an under-18s game the next day and on the off chance I heard the coaches talking about giving him a break as they had eyed him to play for the under-23s the next week. So I let the lad know and he was happy. I did this a lot, the lads trusted me and the way I spoke to the staff meant that they reacted positively to it. However, as a coach you have to see the effects of your actions and anticipate any adverse reactions to what you do and say. I think it is simple but is amazing how many coaches in football are not aware of it!

DEVELOPING INDIVIDUALS

SEE CAPABILITY SECTION 7.

Whether working as part of a team or performing on their own encourage and show people how to take ownership of their career and personal development.

- Clarify their vision.
- Devise a strategy.
- Carry out self-analysis – today versus tomorrow.
- Set some objectives.
- Develop a plan.
- Get the right attitude.
- Build their capability.
- Establish a support structure.
- Create the right image.
- Attain peak performance.

Don't tolerate selfishness.

Team before self. Always.

The power of many is a lot more than the power of one.

Make sure everyone knows it, believes it and acts like it.

'Side before self, every time.'

Billy Bremner

- Leeds United and Scotland captain

REMEMBER YOU ARE DEVELOPING PEOPLE NOT JUST FOOTBALLERS

For people to be happy and successful before, during and after a career in football they need life skills as much as they need ball skills.

Here is an extract from a letter to the young players of Manchester United Academy during the COVID 19 pandemic:

> ***'We can lose track of how lucky we are to be surrounded by an amazing group of talented young individuals. Not just talented football players but talented people. Children who speak languages, write poetry, carry out research, draw, paint, play music, look after Gran, keep fit, make videos, write letters, help their parents around the house, cook a meal, bake a cake, design their own training sessions and invent new skills.***
>
> ***Academies don't measure this stuff. But it is these things that make you who you are. And ultimately it will be these things that make you successful in life. Being yourself and showing the world you are unique is important in a time where it is sometimes easier and desirable for you to conform and fit in with the crowd.***
>
> ***Keep being yourself. You are amazing.'***
>
> **The Academy Staff, Manchester United FC**

Well done Manchester United Academy. This must be so reassuring if you are the parents of one of the players.

Lucy's notebook:

The best young player developer I have worked with was Neil Redfearn at Leeds United. He had the ability to recognise young players' talents and then make them believe in and buy into his plan to make them better players and people. He could be their best friend or worst enemy – that was up to the lads. He was relentlessly onto them about bettering themselves and learning to be better players and people. Neil put the person first and the lads responded to him. He transformed the academy from what it was and produced player after player even in times of dire financial conditions for the club. He created teams at U18 and U23 level which produced individuals who went onto play in the first team at Leeds.

'What makes a good coach? People. Its understanding the person in front of you and their motivation and supporting, guiding and inspiring them to achieve the outcome they want.'

Mark Gannon – chief executive UK Coaching

'You have a duty as a young player developer to maximise everyone in your care whether they are going to 'make it' or not. The result is that even the released players are at a better stage and have the equipment to cope with life whether as a footballer or, more likely, not.

In terms of young player development, the team should be the focus and the individuals will flourish within that structure. Every single one of those lads I coached at Leeds United firmly believed in their place within the structure of those teams. This went a long way to producing professional players.

A lot of clubs just focus on individuals and disregard the rest yet you need a team of players just to produce one first team player so you cannot disregard anyone!'

Neil Redfearn - football player and manager

'The only team that needs to win trophies is the first team. The youth teams don't need to win, they just need to make their players better. Before the age of 14 it's just playful skills and developing good habits, like controlling the ball and passing and positions, and we're thinking a lot about the mental side. So in the end you have not just a complete football player, but a person who is good for others, who means something in the world.'

Dennis Bergkamp - international footballer/ coach talking about Ajax youth development policy

'Where Europe has Ajax Amsterdam, South America has Argentina Juniors. Both clubs stand for two things most of all: a love for the ball and devotion to their youth academies.'

Martin Mazur - BBC Sport

'Football is so much more than just football, it's love, it's passion, it's so much more than kicking a ball. Football unites people. Football changes lives.'

Nor Mustafa – footballer, West Ham Women

INFLUENCE

The Oxford English Dictionary definition is: *The capacity to have an effect on the character or behaviour on someone or something.*

How good are *you* at influencing the way *other people* think?

- Every day your life is affected by thousands of decisions and actions taken by other people including politicians, employers, employees, friends, relatives, colleagues, teammates etc.
- How well they perform directly influences your success and happiness.
- How much influence do you have over their performance?
- Take control.

Everyone is entitled to their views and opinions – respect this.
Whatever you say and do will have an impact on somebody's feelings and emotions – people are human beings not robots.

'You don't get the best out of people by hitting them with an iron rod. You do so by gaining their respect, getting them accustomed to triumphs and convincing them that they are capable of improving their performance.'

Sir Alex Ferguson - football manager

INFLUENCE

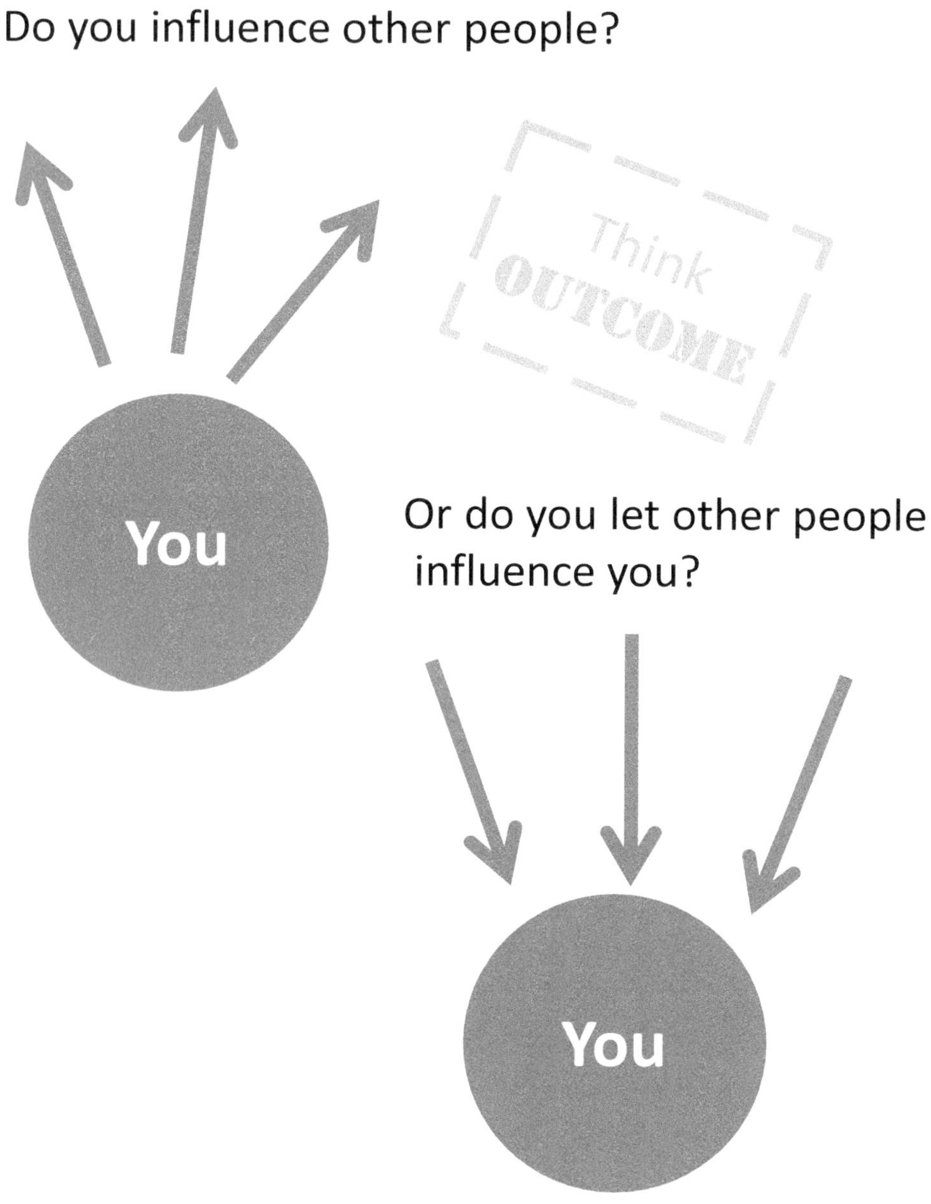
Do you influence other people?
Think
OUTCOME
You
Or do you let other people
influence you?
You

INFLUENCING OTHERS

- Build your knowledge. This will help you influence what other people think.
- There will be some people who are adamant that they don't agree with you. Accept it and move on. Don't waste precious time on them. It is difficult changing someone's attitude towards something if they have strong beliefs.
- Don't waste time trying to influence the wrong people. Work out the people who you want in your world and spend your time with them.
- Use the analogy of heading off on a journey and getting people on your bus, all heading in the same direction.
- There will be those people wanting to get on your bus, those thinking about getting on the bus and those who don't want to join you on your journey.
- Concentrate only on the people already on the bus and those thinking of getting on.
- The very important people in your life are the ones on the bus – look after them.

Influence those who can influence others.

DON'T WASTE TIME TRYING TO INFLUENCE THE WRONG PEOPLE

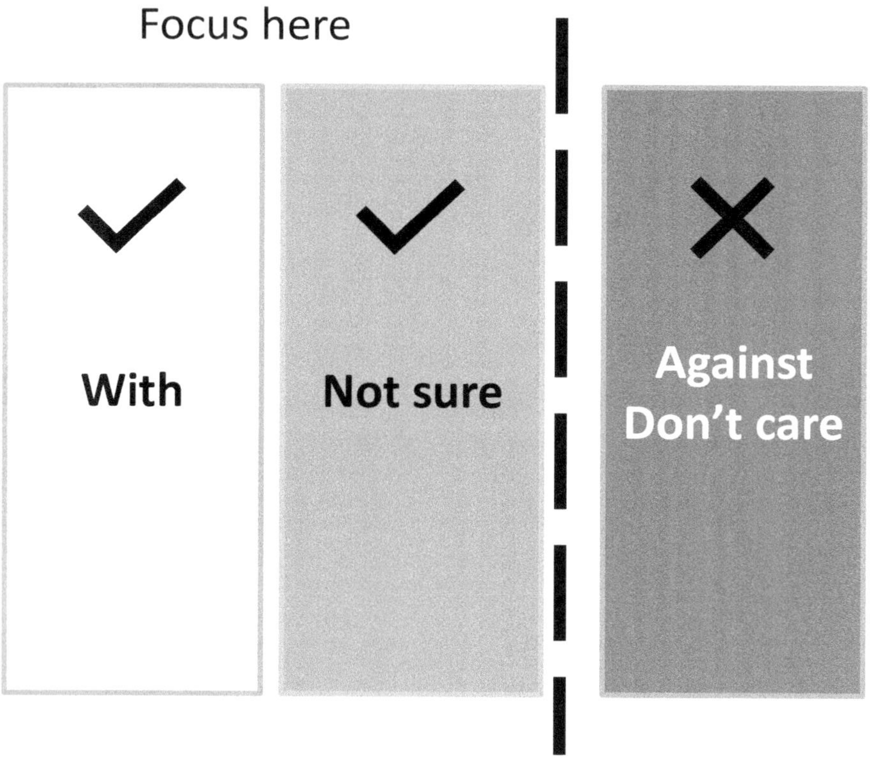

Be really good at dealing with other people.

Most of our lives are spent speaking to, listening to and watching other people.

You need other people to help you be successful.

It makes sense to be great at building relationships and dealing with other people.

BEING INFLUENCED

- You control your thoughts so you decide whether you want to listen to what other people have to say.
- Build your knowledge. This will help you challenge what you are told and you can make up your own mind.
- Think of the source. Is it credible? Do they know what they are talking about?

Here are some simple techniques to stop you being influenced by the wrong people and shield you from hurtful words:

- Think of the words as arrows, put a mental shield around you so that the arrows bounce off without getting through.
- They are just words – If they were uttered in a foreign language you wouldn't understand them anyway.
- Rise above it. Tell yourself that the words don't actually matter. You know what you are doing; dismiss it as if they don't know what they are talking about.

The important point here is that you listen to credible sources, consider the points and decide whether or not you want to be influenced. You stay in control.

> *At any point in time there are people in your life who are influencing the level of your success. Make sure you know who they are. Make sure the influence is positive.*

See Leadership – dealing with opposition.

DEALING WITH CONFLICT

- Don't shy away from the issue because someone is difficult to deal with – that's what they want.
- Losing your temper does not look or sound good. Stay in an adult state – be the grown up not the child.
- Feel interested not threatened – *why do you say that?*
- Even if you don't agree with someone you should still be respectful of their views.
- If someone is rude to you, don't sink to their level by being rude to them.
- Be firm, be honest, say it as it is.
- Don't waffle, be brief and stick to the facts.
- Take away all the emotions and don't indulge in personal criticism.
- Don't try to belittle someone, it will inflame the situation. It does not make you look big by trying to make someone else look small.
- **Problems fester – deal with them promptly.**
- Stay in control, rise above the situation.
- Look at yourself – are you difficult to deal with? Remember people deal with people they like dealing with.

Conflict needs two or more people.
Think about your involvement.
Could you have handled it better?
If it happens a lot then maybe it's you that's the problem.

DEALING WITH OPPOSITION

- Keep things simple – don't over complicate your approach.
- Get to know the opposition.
- Nullify their strengths, exploit their weaknesses.
- Make the opposition worry about you.
- Be in control – always.
- Rise above confrontation.
- Listen only to those with the right knowledge and experience.
- Deal with problems promptly – don't let them fester.
- Enjoy the challenge – make it fun.

Stay positive:

- Moaning adds no value whatsoever.
- If you don't like it do something about it.
- Don't worry about things you can do nothing about.
- Don't worry about people who do not affect your world.
- Negativity is draining.
- Look forward – get excited.
- Don't confuse opposition with people who are genuinely concerned about what you are doing and are only trying to help.

Know your competitors and their strengths and weaknesses.

To be the best you've got to beat the best.

DEALING WITH SETBACKS

- Setbacks happen. They are part of life.
- Step back, take a moment, gather your thoughts, regroup.
- Understand why it's happened and learn from it.
- Stay positive. Don't complain. Don't make excuses.
- Don't blame other people.
- Don't worry about things you can do nothing about.
- See it as a challenge – how will you recover?
- Think OUTCOME – what's the best way forward?
- Look forward; you can't change what's gone.

This is a good way to think about setbacks:

- The chance of encountering setbacks increases according to the number of things you do, the harder you try and the more you push the boundaries. To get setbacks you are out there making things happen – well done!
- The only way to completely eliminate setbacks is to stop doing things – not an option if you want to be the best.
- On the journey to achieving what you want there will be lots of setbacks. This is one of them out of the way and you are a step nearer to achieving your goals.

Don't let anything disrupt the status quo.

When things are going well, keep it that way.

Know what makes you successful and stick to your values, vision and goals.

Be great at spotting trouble.

Be great at dealing with it.

Especially when it's people.

BRIEF NOTES ON MANAGING CHANGE

- To improve performance you have to be prepared to change.
- Change requires a move from one state to another – this particularly applies to your state of mind.
- You need to win the hearts and minds of others – successful change requires the alignment of attitudes of those involved and impacted.
- The ideal starting point is 100 per cent dissatisfaction with the status quo – be mindful that this is unlikely to happen.
- Constant, effective communication is critical.
- Change is disruptive – it needs a great deal of thought to make sure everything has been considered.
- It needs careful planning, including the time needed to bed in.
- Sometimes you will need to take a step backwards in order to take two steps forwards.
- Similarly change can cause a dip in performance before improved performance kicks in. This needs to be managed carefully to prevent it from happening or at least minimise the impact.
- Put monitoring processes in place – stay close to figures, activity and the **people**.

Deal with issues as soon as they arise.

Don't ignore them and hope they'll go away.

Problems fester and get worse.

Why create bigger problems?

THINK IMPACT

- Whenever you do something, it has an impact.
- Think about who and/or what is affected?
- How big is the impact?
- Do you know whether it had a positive or a negative impact?
- Before you took the action did you pre-plan the impact you wanted to make?
- Look at what you are doing every day – are you making an impact?
- Is it the right impact?
- Is it aligned to your strategy – what you want to achieve?
- Link IMPACT to OUTCOME. What outcome do you want? What is the impact being made as a consequence of that outcome?
- How do you measure your impact and that of your team?
- Refer to the Measurement pages in section 5 to get some ideas.
- Think effectiveness, think quality.
- Continually assess what you do and the impact you're making and use the findings to make improvements to your overall performance.

Help people feel good about themselves.

This happens when they:

- *are treated with respect*
- *enjoy what they are doing*
- *know the rules and boundaries*
- *understand the expected level of performance*
- *have the right skills, experience and knowledge*
- *are fairly rewarded*
- *are surrounded by other people who feel good about themselves.*

LOOK AT *EVERYTHING* RELATIVE TO *EVERYTHING ELSE*

- 'Being the best' as a statement assumes relativity to someone. You will only be the winner if you are better than somebody else.
- To win you need to do everything you can to improve your capability and understand the capability of the competition.
- In direct competition your capability will need to include *strategic and tactical skills to beat your opponent (such as exploiting their weaknesses).
- Look at your strengths and weaknesses relative to each other. What's important? Where should I focus?
- Look at your skills relative to each other – which one's contribute most to your performance? Which one's should contribute most?
- Look at your team's performance – best performer?
- Look at your business performance – best area?
- **Look at how you spend your time – is it spent on what's important to you?**

**Strategic is high-level, longer-term planning, tactical is short term, doing things now.*

Think: strategy to win the war, tactics to win the battle.

Think: strategy to win the league, tactics to win the match.

KEY LEADERSHIP TIPS

Be an effective leader.

Successful teams need effective leadership.

Being in charge doesn't make you a leader.

You need to behave like one.

Leadership is not about bossing people around.

Others should follow because they want to, not because they have to.

Build belief in each other.

Believe in yourself.

Help others to believe in themselves.

Get everyone believing in each other.

We are, we can, we will.

Continue to build your leadership skills.

Especially:

- Decision making
- Problem solving
- Handling conflict.

Show your appreciation.

Thank people for doing things.

Politeness is a strength and manners are important.

Don't cheat.

Winning through cheating is not actually winning – it's just cheating.

When you cheat you're telling yourself that you don't think you are good enough to win fairly.

Cheating is for losers.

Lucy's notebook:

It's so important to get it right.

Sadly I worked for my last season in a really toxic environment led and directed by the owner of the club. He revelled in toxic management, pitting staff against one another to see who impressed him the most. It created all sorts of panic and chaos, with previous friends being suspicious of each other and everyone doubting their role in the place. It was an awful time and I would not recommend working under toxic management for any length of time.

Luckily the training ground was shielded to some extent from this, even though we knew what was going on.

'The happier you are, the more likely you are to commit, improve and give something back to the environment that you are in.'

Paul Gustard – former head of rugby, Harlequins

LEADERSHIP IN SUMMARY

KEY THINGS TO GET RIGHT

- Be an *effective* leader.
- Build belief in each other.
- Get people excited about the future.
- Help people feel good about themselves.
- Be accountable for you and your team.
- Have foresight, know what's around the corner.
- Give direction, make decisions.
- Encourage co-operation.

'Leadership is about making people feel good about themselves.'

José Mourinho - football manager

LEADERSHIP IN SUMMARY CONTINUED ...

KEY THINGS TO GET RIGHT

- Fly high, keep an eye on things, swoop low to lend a hand.
- Inspire others through your actions and words.
- Lend support, help, encourage, and be there for people.
- Treat people with dignity and respect.
- Rise above conflict.
- Lead don't boss.
- Be the better person.
- Don't let anything disrupt the status quo.
- Deal with issues as soon as they arise; problems fester.
- Don't cheat.

'I would prefer to lose rather than cheat.'

Marcelo Bielsa - head coach, Leeds United FC

THE ●PEOPLEMAD MODEL

'As a manager you are responsible for the performance of your people. Take ownership and be accountable. Help, support, nurture, coach, LEAD.'

PM

* 9 7 8 1 7 8 0 9 1 6 3 6 1 *

ND - #0131 - 110923 - C0 - 234/156/15 - PB - 9781780916361 - Gloss Lamination